The Novelty Radio Handbook and Price Guide

Debby Weaver

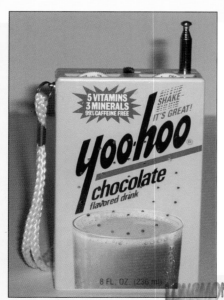

"PUNCHY"

4880 Lower Valley Road, Atglen, PA 19310 USA

Dedication

This book is dedicated to Eileen Weaver. I miss you every day.

Designed by Mark David Bowyer
Type set in Impress BT / Humanist 521 BT

ISBN: 0-7643-2360-1
Printed in China
1 2 3 4

Published by Schiffer Publishing Ltd.
4880 Lower Valley Road
Atglen, PA 19310
Phone: (610) 593-1777; Fax: (610) 593-2002
E-mail: Info@schifferbooks.com

For the largest selection of fine reference books on this and related subjects, please visit our web site at
www.schifferbooks.com
We are always looking for people to write books on new and related subjects. If you have an idea for a book please contact us at the above address.

This book may be purchased from the publisher.
Include $3.95 for shipping.
Please try your bookstore first.
You may write for a free catalog.

In Europe, Schiffer books are distributed by
Bushwood Books
6 Marksbury Ave.
Kew Gardens
Surrey TW9 4JF England
Phone: 44 (0) 20 8392-8585; Fax: 44 (0) 20 8392-9876
E-mail: info@bushwoodbooks.co.uk
Free postage in the U.K., Europe; air mail at cost.

Contents

Acknowledgments

A big thank you to Ray Weaver. He has been collecting and cataloguing his novelty radios for many years. He was also gracious enough to assist in preparing photographs and text for this book. Without Ray, there would not be a "Novelty Radio Nut" ... and no *Novelty Radio Handbook* either.

Thanks to Peter Schiffer and his staff for being so wonderfully kind and encouraging.

Thank you also to my family for giving me the encouragement to keep working on this project: Ken Weaver, Ray and Eileen Weaver, Diane and Chris Atkins, Mandy, Pam, and Michael Kuhn, Ella Weaver, Sandy and Bob Carman, Ed, Bonnie, Sydney, and Callie Weaver.

Finally, writing this book gave me the opportunity to visit my brother, Matt Strock, who lives in the area. Thanks to his boat, we caught many fish. Thanks to his wife, Debbie, we had enough food and drinks to keep us out all day.

Disclaimer and Acknowledgment of Trademarks

Preface

Welcome to the world of novelty radio collecting. Whether you are experienced or a novice in the field of collecting novelty transistor radios, you will find this book useful in assisting you with your endeavors. You will probably recognize some of these radios, and wish you had bought them. Or you may be searching for a specific radio and need to know the average price you should expect to pay. Maybe there are some radios that you didn't know existed, and now you can put them on your Christmas list. This guide will help you, no matter how large or small your collection is.

Collectors have many ways of obtaining their treasures, and having a price guide with photographs is an excellent resource for them. The primary purpose for this book is to identify and evaluate specific novelty radios. The value range provided is based on geographic location, condition, and rarity of the items. There are sometimes exceptions to these values, and neither the author nor publisher can be held responsible for opinions expressed by others regarding prices. No effort has been made to give an *exact* value of the items herein.

Novelty radios, by their own nature, appeal to almost everyone. They come in endless shapes, sizes, and colors. Some radios may use the same exact containers but have a unique decal or detail about them which makes them different. Some radios appear to be identical, but one is AM and the other AM and FM. Some radios are shaped like cars or boats or telephones. Others advertise popular television or cartoon characters.

Novelty radios differ from other radios in that they are poor quality electronic devices. In fact, most have cheaply built speakers driven by the worst electronic equipment available. There are always exceptions, but most of our radios follow the rule, not the exception. Advertisers concerned themselves with appearance and paid little attention to function when producing these radios. Most of the speakers were less than two inches across and produced a "tinny" sound at best. The colorful designs were likeable, but often played with and damaged by children. They were frequently stored away or thrown out. This could explain why such mass produced radios are sometimes hard to locate.

Introduction

Why would anyone dedicate themselves so diligently to collecting something so mundane as a "tinny" sounding piece of plastic which has virtually no intrinsic value and grates on the nerves of its listener? Who knows? But there are many collectors like my father-in-law, Ray Weaver, who have spent a great deal of effort adding to their gallery of these novelty transistor radios. My "Pop's" massive collection of over 1000 examples is a testimony to his devotion to his hobby. When his collection turned into hundreds of these radios, he started keeping records and organizing information about them. I made the remark, "Pop, you're just a Novelty Radio Nut!" He was not offended by the remark. He uses the initials "novrn" as a shortened acronym for "Novelty Radio Nut" on his e-mail address and website. I had also mentioned on another occasion, that he should consider publishing his own collector book. This would give readers an abundance of information along with examples of many radios that do not appear in any other reference books. I was happily surprised when he agreed to provide his knowledge, time, and most importantly, his radios to help *me* write the book.

Pop and I love the radios and make no claims that we know exactly how much they are worth. After over a decade of buying, selling, and researching the radios, we have given the average price you would expect to pay for each. The prices range from a fair example to one that is in mint condition, with no signs of use. Keep these baseline ideas in mind when bargaining with dealers. Sometimes one little book can save you a lot!

As you wander through this unbelievable collection of novelty transistor radios, also keep in mind that these are all really radios, not the product or item that they appear to be. That is what makes them so interesting. You will be amazed at the number of radios that you might have seen or owned throughout your life. Novelty radio collectors know that while some of the radios appear to be identical, they may have subtle differences. Some are AM and FM, and others are AM only. One radio might require a 9 volt battery, while another uses "AA" type batteries. But you don't have to be a "radio nut" to appreciate this collection. The radios provide interest in many areas such as: transportation, food and drink advertising, toys, weaponry, breweriana, and a variety of others.

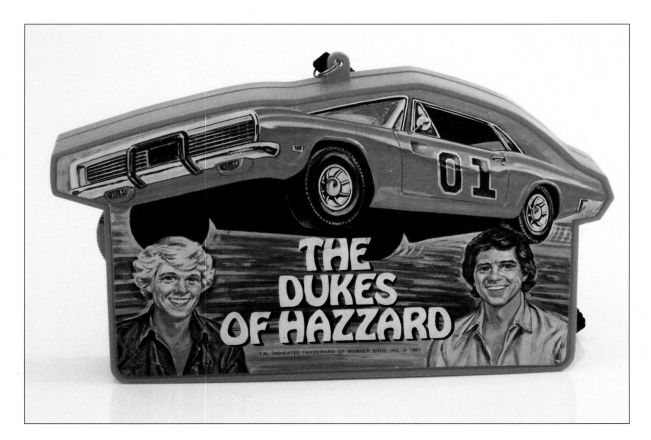

Chapter One

Political and Weaponry

Bicentennial Gas Pump, '76, is an AM radio, made in Hong Kong. It has a carrying strap and measures 4.25" H. $25-40.

Bicentennial Solar is a pocket radio, made in Taiwan. It is brightly colored in red, white, and blue and "76" is written on the front. It measures 5" H and is AM/FM. $40-65.

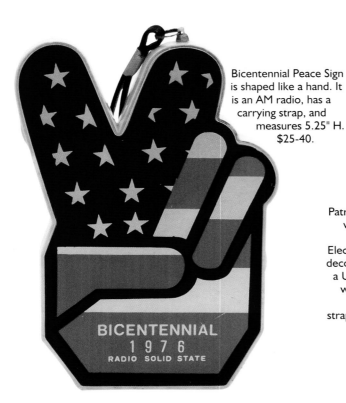

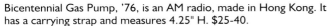

Bicentennial Peace Sign is shaped like a hand. It is an AM radio, has a carrying strap, and measures 5.25" H. $25-40.

Patriotic pocket radio was made in Hong Kong by General Electric®. The radio is decorated to look like a U.S. flag, complete with stars. It has an attached carrying strap and measures 5" H. $25-40.

United We Stand is a scanner radio with no speaker, requiring earphones for use. The radio is a clear, red color with a picture of a U.S. flag on the front. $10-20.

Patriotic Telephone is a large, AM radio, measuring 8.25" H. The receiver is removable, but has no function. The controls are on the sides. This radio was made in Japan. $50-75.

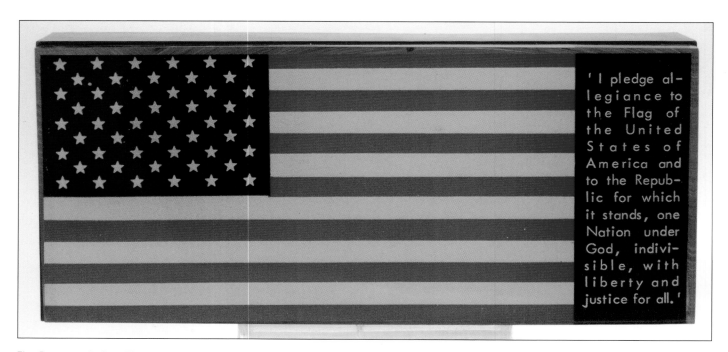

Flag Paperweight has "The Pledge of Allegiance" printed on the front. It is an AM radio made in Hong Kong. The cover is made of lucite and is decorated like a U.S. flag. This radio is 7" L. $30-50.

Cannon is an AM radio. It stands on a plastic frame, with rotating wheels.
The cannon is metal. This radio is 10" L. $35-50.

Hand Grenade was made in Japan and is 5" H. The
trigger and base are metal. The trigger is also a
cigarette lighter. $35-60.

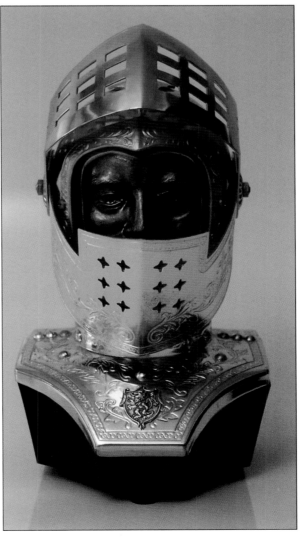

Knight's Helmet
has a visible face
inside. It is plastic
and metal and was
made in Japan.
The shield moves
up and down to
expose the
knight's face. It is
an AM radio and
stands 8.5" H.
$90-115.

9

Knight On Horse stands on a plastic base. It has a removable metal figure of a knight sitting on a horse. This radio was made in Japan and is 9" H. $90-115.

Liberty Bell is 7" H x 7.25" W. The bell shows the crack that appears on the real Liberty Bell. The bell and supports are metal and the base is plastic. $60-85.

Knight Standing has also been called "Man of La Mancha." It is 11.5" H. The metal sword is a removable letter opener. $100-125.

Richard Nixon is a chalk-like figure on a plastic base. Nixon is posed with both hands in the air gesturing peace signs. This AM radio was made in Hong Kong and stands 11" H. $60-100.

Statue of Liberty is an AM radio. Lady Liberty is metal, and stands on a plastic base. This radio was made in Korea. It is large, and measures 12" H and 3.5" W. $50-85.

Spirit of 1776 was made to commemorate the bicentennial in 1976. It has metal figures on a plastic base. The plaque on the front reads, "The United States Of America 1776 1976 Bicentennial." This radio was made in Japan and stands 7.25" H. $75-100.

US Forces Vietnam is a pocket-type, AM radio. It has a drawing of Vietnam and a dragon on the front. There is a large speaker in the center. $35-50.

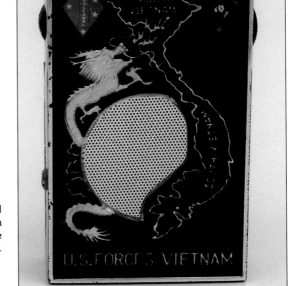

Chapter Two

Sports, Music, and Recreation

American Express® is a credit card-style radio. It is two-sided and is about the size of a credit card. There is an American Express card on one side and a Super Bowl advertisement on the other. $15-25.

Grand National/7-Up® is a two-sided pocket radio. It advertises the Grand National Rodeo on one side and 7-Up on the other. It was made in Hong Kong and is AM. $25-30.

Cotton Bowl Classic is a two-sided, AM, pocket radio. It advertises the Cotton Bowl on one side and KRLD and Kodak on the other side. It was made in China and stands 4.25" H. $25-30.

St. Louis Cardinals/Busch® is a two-sided pocket radio. It has several advertisements, including Kroger® and radio station KMOX on one side and the Cardinals, Busch Beer, and KMOX on the other side. It is AM and measures 3.75" H x 2.5" W. $25-30.

Las Vegas Stars is a two-sided pocket radio. It advertises the Las Vegas Stars and Budget® Used Cars on one side and the Las Vegas Stars and The Wherehouse on the other side. It is an AM radio. $25-30.

Orioles/WCBM is a two-sided pocket radio. It advertises the Orioles and WCBM on one side and the PGA Radio Network on the other. $25-30.

True Value® is an AM pocket radio. It advertises the Chicago Cubs and a local radio station. $15-25.

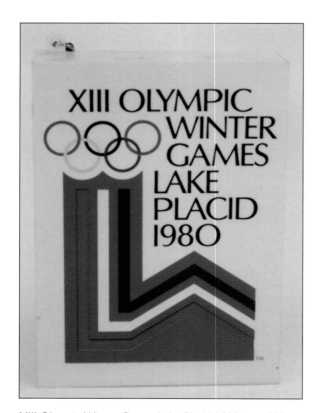

Philadelphia Phillies/National Dairy Month is a two-sided pocket radio. It advertises the Philadelphia Phillies on one side and celebrates the 50th anniversary of National Dairy Month on the reverse side. It is 3.5" H and only 1.25" thick. $25-40.

XIII Olympic Winter Games Lake Placid 1980 is an AM radio. There is an advertisement for the 1980 Olympics on the front, and on the back it advertises Era detergent. $25-30.

Arkansas Razorback is molded plastic and 2-dimensional. It is AM/FM and was made in Hong Kong. It has a swing handle and is 5" H. $45-60.

Baseball and Glove are two radios. The baseball is an FM scanner with a carrying strap. It is 2.5" W. The glove is an AM radio and is molded in the shape of a baseball glove. It is 4.5" H. Baseball is $10-20. Glove is $30-45.

Atlanta Baseball Cap is 3" H and is one of many team caps. It is an AM radio and was made in the USA. $35-60.

Kansas City Baseball Cap is 3" H and is an AM radio. The controls are on the bottom of the cap. It was made in the USA. $35-60.

Baseballs are all alike except for the teams they represent. From left to right they advertise: San Diego Padres, Jacksonville Suns, Dodgers, and Houston. They are AM radios measuring 3.5" H. All have carrying straps. $10-25 each.

Binoculars With Case is an interesting radio, because the binoculars actually work. This radio came with a leather case. It was made in Japan and is 4" H. $40-65.

Bobby Sox Can has a humorous young lady on one side of it and a prayer on the other side. It is 4.75" H. This AM radio was made in Hong Kong. $45-60.

Atlantic City Horse Race Ticket is decorated to look like a race ticket. This is one of a series of similar ticket-types. It is an AM radio and stands 3.5" H. $25-40.

Bay Meadows Horse Race Ticket is decorated to look like a race ticket. The radio advertises, "$50.00, 8th race, win." It is an AM radio and stands 3.5" H. $25-40.

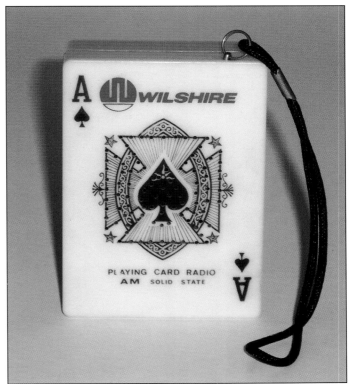

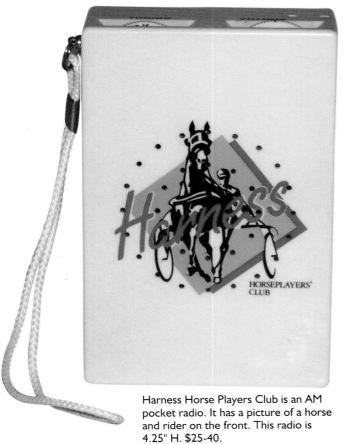

Harness Horse Players Club is an AM pocket radio. It has a picture of a horse and rider on the front. This radio is 4.25" H. $25-40.

Playing Cards is a two-sided radio. One side looks like an Ace of Spades and the other side is a King of Hearts. It is 3.5" H and 2.5" W. $20-35.

Jockey Cap is a small hand-held radio. It is made in the shape of a cap with riding glasses attached. The radio is brightly colored in thick blue and green stripes. The speaker is on the top and the thumbwheel controls are on the back. $20-30.

Football On Stand is an AM radio made for Wilson®. It is 6.5" H. The stand is a kicking tee and is not attached to the ball. Made in Japan. $35-40.

Budweiser® Helmet is shaped like a red football helmet. The speaker is inside the helmet and there is a white "Budweiser" emblem on one side. $45-80.

NFL Football is an AM/FM radio with head-phones. It was packaged with batteries included. $15-25.

Dallas Cowboys is an AM/FM radio shaped like a cube. It is also a clock. It measures 4.5" on all sides. This radio was made in Hong Kong. $35-60.

Decision Maker Game has a switch to turn on the "yes" or "no" lights and a button that causes one light to go out, making the "yes" or "no" decision for you. It stands 3.5" H and was made in Japan. $35-50.

Chess Set has actual chess pieces cut in half and mounted in the plastic. This radio was made in Hong Kong and measures 7" L x 2" H. $50-65.

Roulette Wheel is an AM/FM radio. It looks like a real roulette wheel, complete with a large, red and black, numbered center. The top of the wheel says, "Paradice Hotel Casino." $50-65.

Pool Table is an AM/FM radio made in the shape of a pool table. This radio has a ball rack that controls the volume and cue stick used for tuning. Standing upright it measures 7" H and 4.75" W. $50-85.

Roulette Wheel Game measures 5" H and 5.25" W. It came with a game board and chips. A push-button on the side spins the wheel. This radio/game was made in Japan. $100-125.

Dice Game has dice that light up when the play button is pushed. Pushing the stop button gives your points. A playing board came with this radio. It was made in Japan. $40-65.

Red Dice radio is an AM radio. It has a large tuning dial on one side, with "Sanyo"® printed in the center. It was made in Japan and measures 3.25" square. The controls are on the top. $20-35.

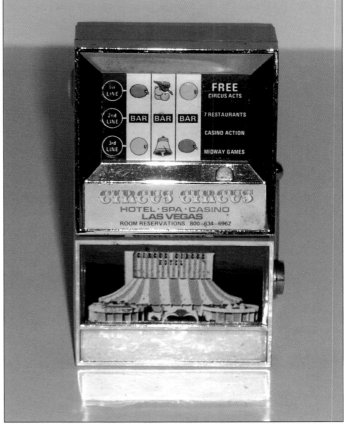

Black Dice is an AM radio shaped like a large black die. It is 3.25" square. The controls are on one side. $25-35.

Slot Machine is an AM radio. It is shaped like a slot machine and the front says, "Circus Circus." This radio was made in Hong Kong and measures 4.25" H and 2.5" W. $25-40.

Golf Ball On Stand is a thin, wafer-type radio. It is 3.25" H and is usable with earphones only, which can be stored in the radio's right side. It came with an attached belt clip. $15-30.

Wilson Tennis Ball Can is smaller than a can of tennis balls. It measures only 4.75" H. It is an AM radio made in Hong Kong. It is plastic with a paper label. $25-40.

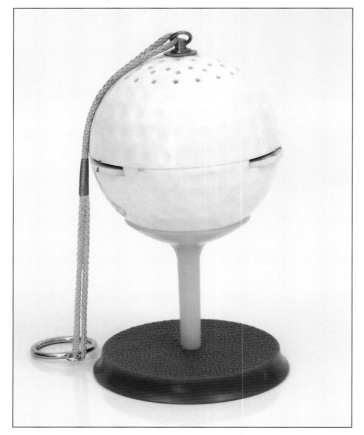

Golf Cart is an AM radio. The cart is metal and holds a plastic golf bag. The clubs are removable. This radio is 7.25" H and was made in Japan. $50-85.

Golf Ball On Tee is 5.25" H, with the ball on the tee. The ball contains the radio, and can be removed from the tee, which is easily lost. It is an AM radio made in Japan. $60-85.

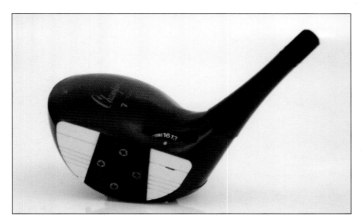

Golf Club has a volume control at the tip of the handle. It stands 4.5" H. It is an AM radio made in Japan. $50-75.

Roller skate is an AM radio. It was made in Hong Kong and distributed through Prime designs. It has a UK registration number on it. This radio is shaped like a blue roller skate with yellow wheels. It stands 6" H. $20-45.

Golfer Award Trophy has a plate for engraving on the front. There is a figure on the top of the radio swinging a golf club. This radio is 6.5" H and was made in Japan. $35-50.

Phonograph with Nipper is an AM radio and a jewelry box. It was made in Japan and measures 5" H and 6.5" L. The lid can be removed for storage. $85-110.

RCA Nipper with Chipper is an AM/FM pocket-size radio. It is red with the "Nipper" and "Chipper" figures on the front. $25-40.

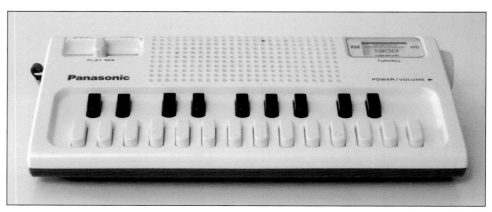

Organ Keyboard by Panasonic® is an AM radio that looks like a keyboard. This radio plays music while you play the keyboard. It was made in Japan and is 8.5" L. $40-55.

Country Music Jug has graphics on both sides. One side has a "Country Music" decal and the other side has a decal with different instruments pictured. It was made in Japan and is 5.2" H. $50-75.

Fender® Guitar radios are the same, except one is blonde and the other is red. They can only be used with earphones plugged into the Fender amp. These guitars were made in China and stand 13" H. $75-100.

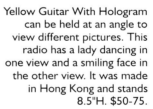

Stellar® Guitar is an AM radio made in Japan. It is 12" H. This radio is made in the shape of an acoustic guitar. $40-60.

Yellow Guitar With Hologram can be held at an angle to view different pictures. This radio has a lady dancing in one view and a smiling face in the other view. It was made in Hong Kong and stands 8.5"H. $50-75.

Nashville Picker Guitar is an AM radio painted red, white, and blue. The strings make sounds when strummed. It was made in Hong Kong. $60-80.

Chapter Three

Transportation with Parts and Accessories

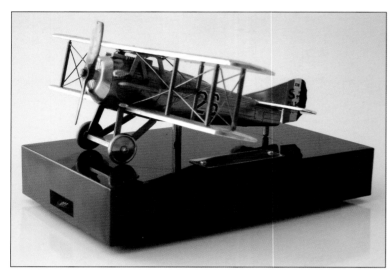

Biplane is an AM radio. The plane is metal and sits on a plastic base. It has an 8" wingspan and measures 6.75" in length. This radio was made in Hong Kong. $75-110.

KLM® Airplane is a very small AM radio. It measures 2.5" long with a wingspan of 2.25". This radio requires earphones for use. The tuner is on top of the cockpit and a belt clip is on the bottom of the airplane. $10-20.

TWA® 747 Airplane is a nice looking display piece. It measures 13" L with a wingspan of 12.5". It is an AM radio made in Hong Kong. $125-160.

Space Shuttle Columbia is pictured without the plastic stand that came with it. The value reflects the price without the stand. It is 10" L and has a wingspan of 6.5". This AM radio was made in Hong Kong for Radio Shack. $30-60.

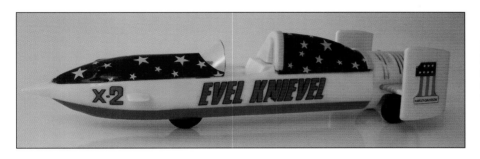

Evel Knievel's X-2 Rocket-Cycle is an interesting cross-collectible. It is plastic with stickers advertising Harley Davidson. It is an AM radio and measures 12.5" L. Even in poor condition this is a very desirable novelty. $100-130.

Evel Knievel on a Harley® is another great find for a collector. Even with the damage to the outside of this pocket-sized radio, it is worth having. This AM radio is 5" W and has a handy carrying strap. The controls are above the front wheel and the top of Evel's head. $80-100.

Cabin Cruiser is plastic with some metal on the edges. The cruiser has a removable lifeboat with many other realistic details, such as an anchor, lamps, a horn, and visible instruments. It was made in Japan and is 11.5" L and 6.5" H. $55-90.

Motorcycle with Harley Davidson® stickers was probably a generic, with the stickers added later. It is 11.5" L and was made in China. The tuner and volume controls are on the rear tire of this FM radio. $30-45.

Santa Maria represents a combination of a plastic base with metal trim and cloth sails and flags. It gives the ship a very authentic look but makes it difficult to keep clean. The radio is AM and was made in Japan. It measures 11.5" L and 11" H. $65-100.

Red 1957 Chevrolet® Corvette is a common AM/FM radio made in China. The controls are under the hood of the car. It measures 8.5" L. $15-25.

Yellow 1955 Ford® Thunderbird is another common AM/FM radio made in China. The car is a convertible and the top is removable. It measures 10" L and the hood lifts, revealing the controls. $15-25.

Mississippi Fire Pumper is a replica of an 1869 unit. It is metal with some plastic and has removable hoses, which are often lost. This radio was made in Japan and is 10.25" L and 6.5" H. $80-100.

The 1966 Buick® Riviera is a plastic replica with controls on the bottom. It has nice details including the hidden headlights and opposing windshield wipers that were on this model year. The radio is AM only, made in Japan, and requires one 9 volt battery to operate. $50-75.

The 1967 Chevrolet Camaro is unusual because the car is sitting on a base which contains the radio. The plastic car is not a radio, but displays well on its wooden base. The car is 7" L and the base is 11.5" L. $85-110.

The 1965 Oldsmobile® Delta 88 has a plastic body with controls on the bottom. It is another AM radio made in Japan. It measures 9" L and operates with one 9 volt battery. $60-85.

The 1965 Pontiac® Grand Prix is another one of the made in Japan plastic cars. It measures 9" L and requires one 9 volt battery to operate. The car is an AM radio with all the super details that made this car a classic. $50-75.

Dale Earnhardt Racecars are small and large examples of the same radios. The cars have the #3 and the sponsor's graphics on them. They are both AM/FM and are made in China. The large car is 6.5" L and the controls are on the bottom. The small car is 4.5" L and the controls are on the side windows. $60-85 each.

Dale Earnhardt Jr. Racecar displays the #8 and graphics on the body. It is a small 4.5" L car made in China. The controls are located on the side windows. $60-85.

Mark Martin Racecar is another of the series of racecars made in China. This car is 6.5" L and is also AM/FM. The car displays well, with the #6 and great advertising covering it. The earphone jack is visible above the rear driver's side tire. $60-85.

Jeff Gordon Racecar is a large example exactly like the Dale Earnhardt 6.5" L car. It has the #24 and Dupont advertising, just like the real racecar. The controls are on the bottom and it is made in China. $60-85.

This 1931 Rolls Royce® Collection pictures several examples of the many versions of this radio. There are metal and plastic examples and they were produced in places like Japan, China, and Hong Kong. The Japanese cars are more detailed than the others, but they all display well. Companies redesigned the cars, removing the hood ornament feature (which was easily broken), and changed the grills. These cars range in price from $20-50.

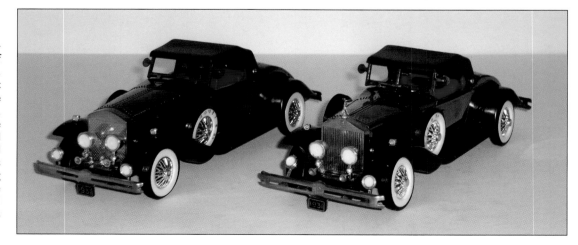

More 1931 Rolls Royce Cars are pictured. The red and pink car has a broken hood ornament and metal running boards. The black and tan car has no hood ornament and plastic running boards. The red and white cars do not have hood ornaments. All cars are about 10" L and 3.5" W. $20-50.

Yellow and Green Rolls Royce Cars are the same design as the previous cars. Both have broken hood ornaments. This series of cars has tuner and volume controls located on the spare tires on both sides. All cars are AM radios. The pewter and gold cars show different running boards and give the profile view. $20-50.

Corgi® Radio Van is made of die cast metal and advertises "RTL 208" on both sides. The van also says "Luxembourg" but is made in Great Britain by Corgi Toys. It measures 4.75" L and 2.4" H. $35-50.

Trotters Car® has only 3 wheels. The front wheel is the tuner for this Chinese-made car. It is AM/FM and measures 8" L. $45-60.

VW® Bug is a fairly new, mass-produced radio, made in China. The car is 9" L and is AM/FM. $20-35.

Michelin® Man was made in Italy. This example is AM, unlike the AM/FM version that has an antenna on the right side and an off/on light in the front. This radio is molded plastic and is 6.5" H. $200-350.

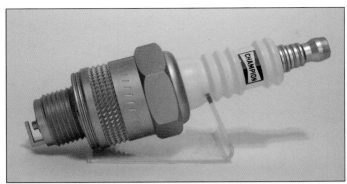

Champion® Spark Plug is an AM/FM radio. The high voltage connection is the volume control, and the threads on the base are the tuner. This radio was made in Hong Kong and is 9.5" L. $40-50.

Michelin Tire is plastic with an attached carrying strap. The thumbwheel controls are on the front of the tire. The word "Michelin" is printed in large letters near the bottom. $20-35.

Harley Davidson Clip-on is an AM/FM radio. It requires earphones for use and has a large belt clip attached to the back. It measures just 4" L. $20-35.

Gearshift is an FM scanner made in China. The volume and tuning controls are in the shifter. This radio measures 4" H and 3.5" W. $20-35.

Monroe® Shock Absorbers is a can-type radio with a swinging trash can lid. It is an AM radio and was made in Hong Kong. The controls are located on the sides. $45-60.

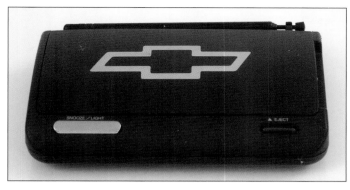

The Chevrolet Logo on this radio makes it a novelty. It is also an alarm clock. The radio is AM/FM and the lid closes for traveling. It measures about 4.5" W. $30-40.

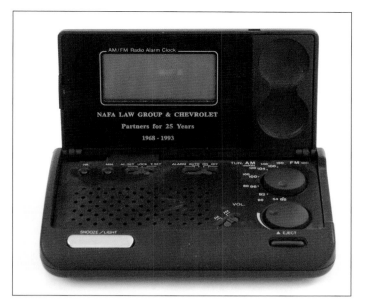

Goodyear® Road Rescue is a weather radio made in Hong Kong. It advertises "Goodyear Tires" and measures 4" H and 3.5" W. $20-35.

AC® Oil Filter advertises the Duraguard Filter by AC on its label. It is an AM/FM radio made in China. It measures 4" H. $35-50.

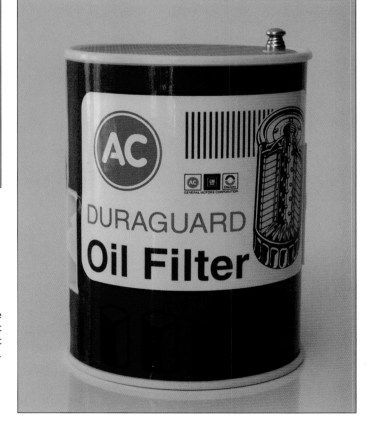

Mack® Oil Filter is a molded plastic radio with the Mack bulldog pictured on the front. The back of the radio has installation instructions for the filter. It was made in Hong Kong and measures 4" H. $50-65.

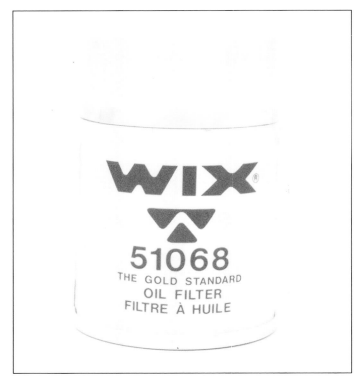

Wix® Oil Filter was made in Canada. The label is printed in French and English. It measures 4.5" H. $30-45.

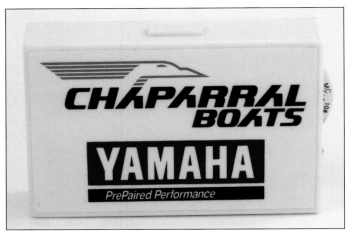

Chapparal Boats is a pocket radio featuring "Yamaha"® on the label. This radio is also made with a black background. $20-35.

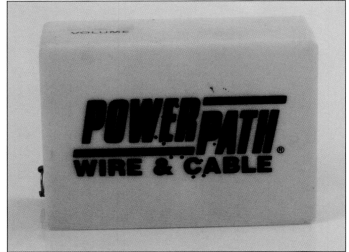

Green Light Auto®/Power Path® Wire and Cable is a pocket radio with two sides of advertising. It is AM and measures 4" L. The carrying strap is missing on this example. $15-25.

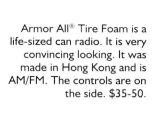

Armor All® Tire Foam is a life-sized can radio. It is very convincing looking. It was made in Hong Kong and is AM/FM. The controls are on the side. $35-50.

Rust-oleum® is a life-sized can depicting this Metal Primer's features on the can. This radio was made in Hong Kong and is also available with a gold cap. $35-50.

Enco® Extra is a gas pump style AM radio. It is shaped like a gas pump and has a picture of a tiger on the front. It measures 4.5" H. $25-40.

STP® Oil Treatment can is a life-sized copy of the product. The speaker is in the lid and the controls are on the sides. The radio pictured advertises "The Racer's Edge" version of the oil treatment, but there is another label for the product advertising a "Secret Formula." $35-50.

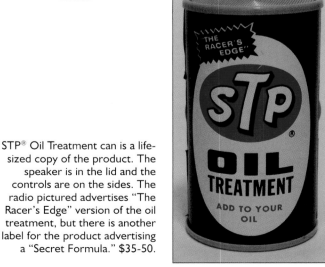

Kendall® GT-1 Racing Oil is an AM radio depicting the motor oil. The label has racing flags across the top and "Pennsylvania" written on the bottom. $30-60.

Havoline® Super Premium motor oil is an interesting can radio. When turned around, the back label has a picture of Bob Hope and an advertisement for one of his shows. The can has "Texaco" printed on both sides. $35-50.

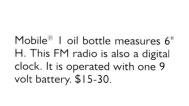

Super 2000® Motor Oil bottle is a large radio measuring 8.5" H. The tuner on this radio is located on the bottom and the off/on is the cap. It was made in China. $25-40.

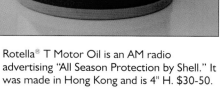

Rotella® T Motor Oil is an AM radio advertising "All Season Protection by Shell." It was made in Hong Kong and is 4" H. $30-50.

Mobile® 1 oil bottle measures 6" H. This FM radio is also a digital clock. It is operated with one 9 volt battery. $15-30.

Chapter Four

Gadgets, Gizmos, and Doo-Dads

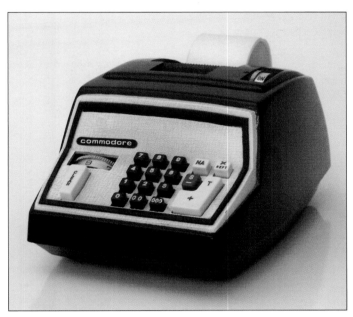

Adding Machine is an AM radio. It was made by Commodore® in Japan. The machine looks real, but is not functional. It is only 3" H and holds a roll of paper. $60-85.

Armillary Sphere is a replica of an ancient astronomy device. There is a blank plate on the bottom for engraving. The radio is AM and made of metal. It measures 7.75" H. $75-110.

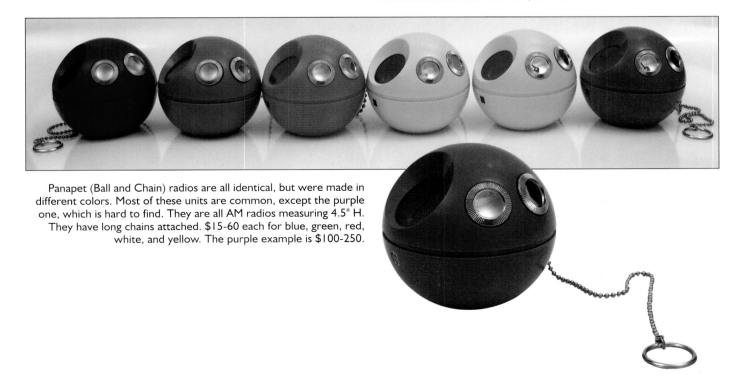

Panapet (Ball and Chain) radios are all identical, but were made in different colors. Most of these units are common, except the purple one, which is hard to find. They are all AM radios measuring 4.5" H. They have long chains attached. $15-60 each for blue, green, red, white, and yellow. The purple example is $100-250.

Ball radios are small, measuring only 2.5" W each. They were mass-produced in China and are all valued the same. Each one is AM/FM. $15-30.

Six-pack Of Beer radio is only 3.5" H and 3.75" W and comes with a bottle opener on the side. The antenna, tuner, and off/on controls are individual bottle caps. This radio is AM/FM. $15-25.

Camcorder Junior is an AM/FM radio with an attached carrying strap. The camera's lens is the volume knob. This unit is 7" L and 4.5" H. $35-50.

Ceramic Cathedral radio has plastic knobs and back with a ceramic front. It stands 9" H and is AM/FM. There are numerous cathedral type radios, but most are plastic. This unit was made in China. $30-45.

Calendar radio has a flip-over date holder. It is an AM radio and stands 5" H. The radio is colored black and white. There is a decal on the bottom left corner that reads "Stewart." $20-35.

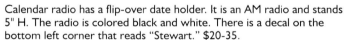

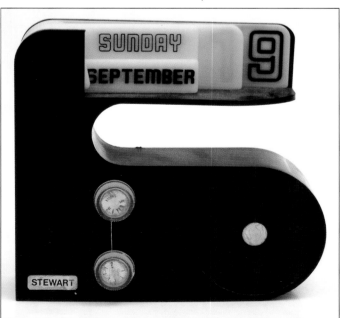

Fantasia Light Radio is aptly named. It has a button on the front that will either turn on the lights or the radio. "Fantasia Radio" is printed near the bottom. This radio is AM only. $30-45.

Hit Tunes radio came in a variety of colors. This AM/FM radio was made in China. This round radio is white with a large, blue circle in the center. It measures 6" across. $15-25.

Italian Chalet radio has a duplicate clock available. The radio is pictured on the right, with the clock on the left, for comparison. This FM radio was made in China. Both chalets measure 4.5" H and 5" L. $85-110.

Jukebox radio with cassette player is 11" H. It was made in Korea and marked #1-9873. There are large buttons on the front that control the cassette player. $60-80.

Classic Tunes Jukebox radio was made in China. It is AM/FM and measures 6.25" H and 6" W. This unit is all molded plastic. This radio looks like an old jukebox that sat on cafeteria tables. $10-25.

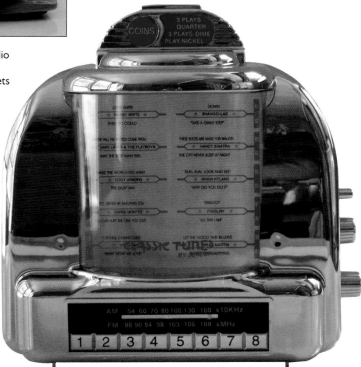

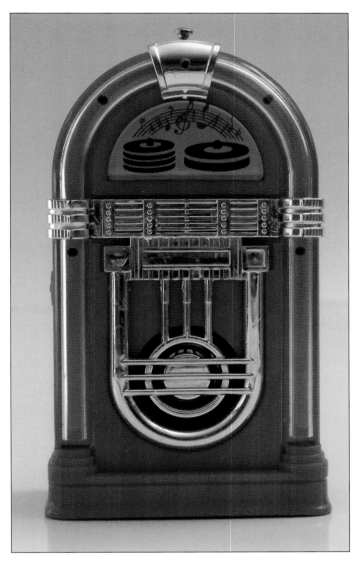

Lamppost is shaped like a lamppost with a large eagle on the top. There is a thermometer in the center of the eagle. This radio has a thumbwheel on the front of the base. $25-40.

Jukebox Mini is a red example of this radio, which came in many colors. It is AM/FM and lights up when playing. The radio stands 5.5" H. $15-25.

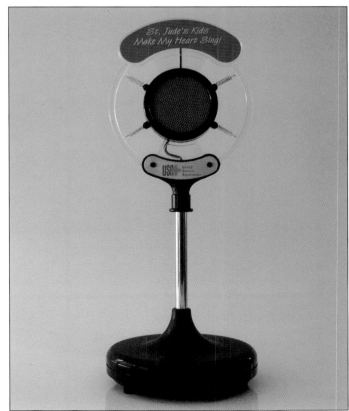

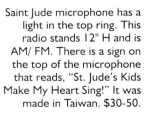

Saint Jude microphone has a light in the top ring. This radio stands 12" H and is AM/ FM. There is a sign on the top of the microphone that reads, "St. Jude's Kids Make My Heart Sing!" It was made in Taiwan. $30-50.

Personal Computer is an FM scanner. This radio is 4.5" H and the mouse is used to change the station. $10-25.

Personal Computer by Lifelong® is another of this series of PC's. This unit has no mouse and functions as an AM/FM radio. $10-25.

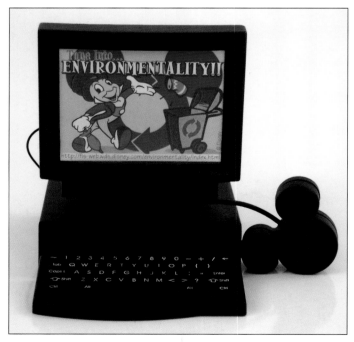

Personal Computer with Jiminy Cricket on screen is an FM scanner. The mouse is shaped like a mouse head with ears and changes the station. $10-25.

Personal Computer by Zorix® is similar in size and function to the previous Lifelong PC. This unit has a mouse that functions as the tuner. $10-25.

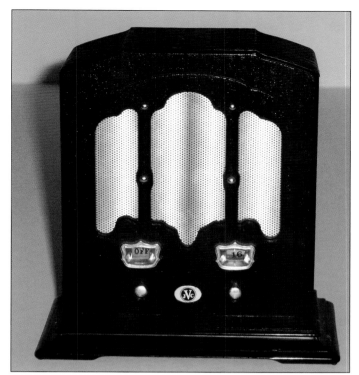

Tombstone-style JVC® Radio has a jewelry box under the lid. It is an AM radio and was made in Japan. It stands 5.5" H. $25-40.

Radio by Classic® is a new replica of an old style radio. This unit was mass-produced in China and is AM/FM. $15-25.

Presentation Key by Solid State® is a large example measuring 14" H. There is a plate on the key for engraving. This radio is metal with a plastic faceplate. It was made in Japan. $45-60.

Yellow Robot radio is also known as "Starroid IR12." It was made in Hong Kong and stands 8.25" H. This robot has flashing, lamp eyes that follow sound. $50-65.

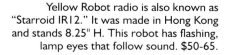

45

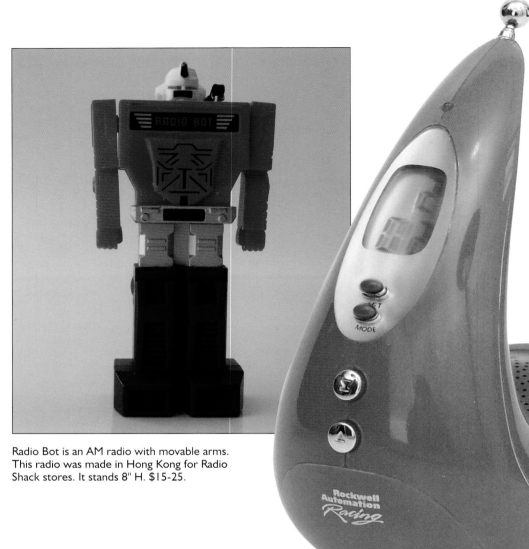

Radio Bot is an AM radio with movable arms. This radio was made in Hong Kong for Radio Shack stores. It stands 8" H. $15-25.

Rockwell® Automation is a scanner radio with a digital clock display. It is red with the logo "Rockwell Automation Racing" on the front. It stands 6" H and was made in China. $10-25.

Safe Bank radio is an AM radio with a large tuning knob decorating the front. This unit was made in Hong Kong and sold at K-mart®. It stands 5" H. $35-50.

Robot radio has a handle on the top that looks metal, but is plastic. This radio is an FM scanner made in China. It is 4.5" H. $15-25.

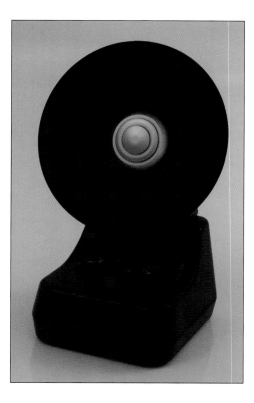

Satellite Dish radio was made in Taiwan. It is shaped like a satellite dish. This radio is AM/FM and measures 7.5" H and 4.75" W. $20-35.

Smoker Sound Stereo has a lid that opens, with a lighter inside and a compartment for cigarettes. It looks like an old console stereo from the 1960s and 1970s. It measures 9" W and 5" H. $15-30.

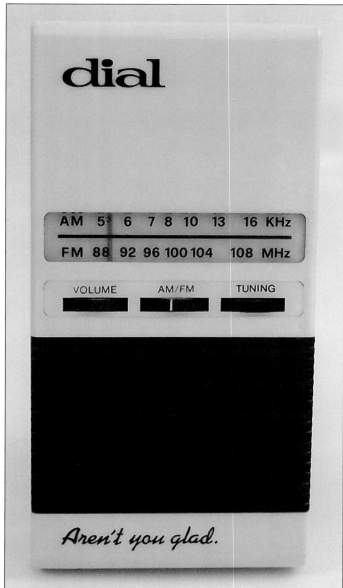

dial

AM 5³ 6 7 8 10 13 16 KHz

FM 88 92 96 100 104 108 MHz

VOLUME   AM/FM   TUNING

Aren't you glad.

Square D Circuit Breaker radio is AM/FM and looks like a real circuit breaker. It is 7" L. The breaker switch turns the radio off and on. $45-65.

Dial® Shower radio brags on the front "Aren't You Glad." It is AM/FM and was made in Taiwan. This is a large unit measuring 10" H and 5" W. $25-40.

47

The Strapper by Randix® has a belt clip on the back for use when exercising. This radio has a large tuning dial on the front with the word "Randix" printed above it. It is an AM radio and stands 5" H. $15-25.

Reel-to-Reel Tape Recorder radio measures 5.5" H with the lid opened. Its reels rotate when selecting the station. It is AM/FM. $45-60.

Tape Deck radio has a lamp inside that flashes when music is played. It was made in Hong Kong. The reels are movable and function as controls. It measures 5.75" H and 6" W. $30-50.

Switchit radio came with a necklace that was used as an antenna. It also had a clear case. This radio has lights that flash when playing. It is 2.5" W and is AM/FM. $40-50.

Candlestick Telephone is 9.5" H. This radio uses the switch hook to turn it on, the mouthpiece controls the volume, and the dial works the tuner. It was made in Korea for Radio Shack. $20-40.

Cellular Telephone is blue and is one of a series of different colors. This AM/FM radio is also a calculator with a flip-top. It measures 7.5" L when opened. $20-35.

French-style Telephone was made in Japan. It has a cigarette lighter built into the receiver. This radio measures 6.5" H and 6" W. $35-60.

Telephone Calculator is a burgundy-colored radio. It is 6" L. This radio is AM/FM and reads "Kaiwa"® on the front. $25-40.

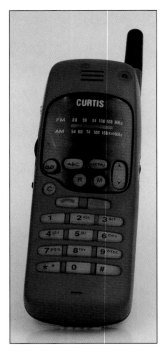

Cellular Telephone is green. It was made by Curtis® and can be used with earphones. This AM/FM radio has an attached belt clip. $20-35.

Console Television radio has a picture frame behind the clear screen, so you can change the photo inside. The top lifts up to reveal a jewelry box. This radio is 5" H and was made in Japan. $25-40.

Princess Telephone radio was made by Solid State. It has a speaker in the receiver for personal listening. This radio was made in Japan. The tuning is operated by the dial and the thumbwheel is the volume control. This radio comes in many different colors. $45-60.

Business Phone radio has a tuning knob on top of the dial. It is white with a removable receiver. It is an AM radio made in Japan. $45-60.

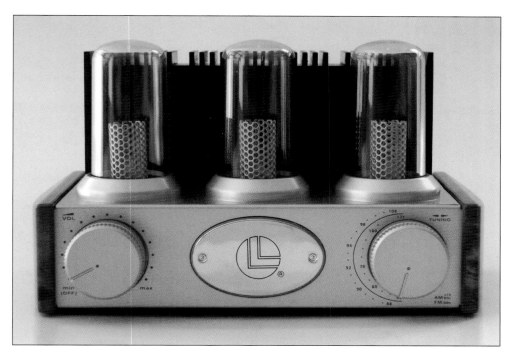

Tube-type radio has tubes that glow when it is played. It is AM/FM and measures 6" L. This unit was made in China. $20-35.

Turntable radio has a moving lid that opens and closes. The knob on the left rotates the turntable and functions as a tuner. This radio is 6" W and was made in China. $20-35.

Wall Clock radio was made by Westinghouse®. It measures 12.5" H and 8.5" W. It is wall-mountable and the controls are hidden on the bottom under the cover. $35-50.

Wall Outlet radio is difficult to spot as a radio. It looks exactly like an outlet and is powered by an AC line. This is an AM radio and measures 6.5" L. $45-65.

Waterwheel House radio is a rare example of a 2-transistor model. It was made in Japan and is 7" L. The tuning wheel clearly displays the fact that it is an AM radio. $100-140.

World Globe radio was made by Tandy®. It is a good-looking, rotating globe and an AM radio. It was made in Korea and stands 8" H. $35-50.

Chapter Five

Food Advertising

Austin® Quality Foods is a small box radio with an attached carrying strap. It measures 3" H and 4.25" L. This radio is AM/FM. $55-80.

Adolph's® Meat Tenderizer is a can-type radio, and stands 4.75" H. The tuner and volume thumbwheels are located on the sides of this radio. The speaker is on the top. It is AM/FM, made in Hong Kong. $30-60.

Arm and Hammer® Baking Soda is the actual size of the real product. A green stripe on the left side contains printing that reads, "A House-Full Of Uses!" It is 4" H and has an attached carrying strap. $35-50.

Betty Crocker® Chocolate Frosting is the actual size of the real product. The tuning and volume knobs are on the sides. This radio was made in Hong Kong. $35-50.

Cookie Crisp® is a box radio made of plastic with a paper label. It is 4.75" H. This AM radio was made in Hong Kong. $50-75.

Bubble Tape® Bubble Gum is an actual-sized radio. It can only be played with earphones and is FM. This radio is dated 1995 and comes with a carrying strap and belt clip. It was made in China and measures 3" W. $20-30.

Kellogg's® Frosties/Ricicles is a two-sided radio that advertises both Kellogg's products. The Frosties side reads "Kellogg Company, 1969" on the bottom. This AM radio was made in Hong Kong and is 3.75" H. $25-40.

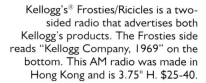

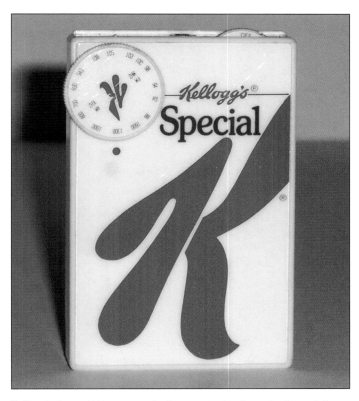

Delmonte® Pineapple Spears is an actual size can-type radio. It is AM and requires a 9 volt battery for operation. This radio was made in Hong Kong and is 3.5" H. $50-75.

Kellogg's Special K has a nice looking tuning knob on the front, left side with a large "K" printed in the middle. It was made in China and is AM/FM. It is 4" H. $20-35.

Canfield's® Diet Chocolate Fudge Soda is the size of a soda can. The speaker is located on the top of the can. $35-50.

Tony The Tiger is a brightly colored radio. It is dated 1980. The name "Tony" is printed under the molded figure of Tony the Tiger. It was made in Hong Kong and measures 7" H and 4" W. $30-45.

Ice Cream Bar radio is dated 1977 and measures 7" L. It looks like an ice cream bar with a bite taken out of it. This radio was made in Hong Kong. $50-75.

Hershey's® Syrup bottle has a removable lid. It is the same size as the real product, and is decorated exactly like it. This AM radio was made in Hong Kong and measures 8.5" H. $60-75.

Ice Cream Cone radio is dated 1977 and measures about 7" L with the base. It is shaped like an ice cream cone. This radio was made in Hong Kong. $50-75.

Kemp's® Fruit Twirlers/ Kemp's Sundae Toppers is a two-sided can radio. It advertises these two Kemp's products. It was made in China and measures 4" H. This radio is AM/FM. $35-50.

Sta-Puff man has a switch on the front that turns on a light. This radio has a white, puffy figure standing on a green base. It was made for the movie *Ghostbusters*. This radio was made in China and stands 7.5" H. $15-30.

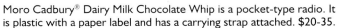

Moro Cadbury® Dairy Milk Chocolate Whip is a pocket-type radio. It is plastic with a paper label and has a carrying strap attached. $20-35.

Durkee® French Fried Onions is a life-sized can radio. It was made in Hong Kong and is AM only. This radio is 4.75" H and requires one 9 volt battery to operate. $35-50.

Strawberry is another molded plastic radio with plastic leaves. It is about 6" H with a carrying strap. $20-35.

French's® Automash Potato Mix is a can-type radio. The tuner and volume controls are on the sides and the speakers are on the top of this life-sized unit. $30-50.

Treesweet® Orange has a large tuning dial on the front with "Treesweet" printed on it. The dial has three cute oranges pictured. It was made in Hong Kong and measures 3.5" W. $25-60.

Green Apple is about the size of a real apple, measuring 4.5" H. This Hong Kong radio has a plastic body and leaves. $15-30.

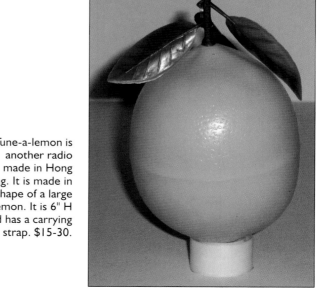

Tune-a-lemon is another radio made in Hong Kong. It is made in the shape of a large lemon. It is 6" H and has a carrying strap. $15-30.

Gulden's® Mustard is an AM radio made in Hong Kong. It is difficult to tell this unit from the actual product. It measures 5.25" H. The metal lid is removable, exposing the battery compartment. $60-80.

Sunbelt® Chewy Granola is a pocket-sized radio measuring 4.5" H. It is dated 1985-87 and is AM/FM. This radio has advertisements of the company's other products on the reverse side. $50-65.

Hamburger is another Hong Kong-produced radio. It was distributed by Amico®, Windsor®, and Sears®. It has an attached carrying strap and measures 6" W and 2.5" H. $15-25.

Nature Valley® Granola is an AM radio made in Hong Kong. It is 4.75" H and has its product information on all sides of the box. $50-65.

Hamburger Helper Hand is an AM radio that was offered by General Mills® to advertise their product, Hamburger Helper. They also made a molded plastic clock that looks almost identical to the radio. This radio was made in Hong Kong and stands 6.5" H. The red nose in the center of the hand controls the volume. $45-65.

Heinz® Baked Beans is a can-type radio made in Hong Kong. This radio is FM only. It is a British design with a blue paper label. It is 4.5" H. $45-60.

Heinz Mexican Style Ketchup is the same radio as the Heinz Tomato Ketchup, but advertises a different Heinz product. It has a different paper label advertising the "Mexican Style Ketchup." $50-75.

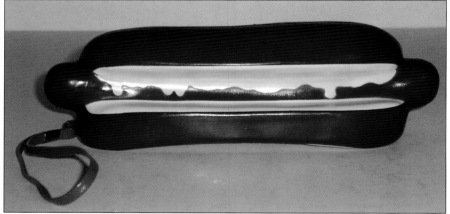

Hotdog radio is rarer than the Hamburger, but makes a good looking mate for it. This radio was made in Hong Kong and is a life-sized 8.25" L and 2.5" H. $25-40.

Heinz Tomato Ketchup looks like a real bottle of ketchup. It is an AM radio and is 8" H. The volume control is under the cap. This unit was made in Hong Kong for Radio Shack and requires two "AA" batteries. $50-75.

Hunt's® Manwich Sloppy Joe Sauce is an AM/FM radio made in Hong Kong. It is very life-like, with cooking directions on the back of the label. $35-50.

Jollibee With Ball is an FM only radio. The Jollibee character is holding a basketball. This unit is 5" H. $45-60.

Jollibee® French Fries is an AM/FM radio and stands 7.5" H. The antenna, tuner, and volume controls are individual French fries in the box. $45-60.

Kraft Macaroni and Cheese Dinner is an AM/FM radio made in China. This radio is a little bigger than the Kraft Dinner radio, 4.5" H. $30-50.

Kentucky Fried Chicken® is a two-sided radio with a picture of Colonel Sanders on one side and Korean printing on the other side. This radio was made in Korea and is 5.25" H. $45-60.

Krystal® radio advertises "New Chili Pups" for their fast food chain. It is small, only 2.25" H and 3.5" L. It was made in China and requires earphones for use. $20-35.

Kraft® Dinner radio is the Canadian version of the U.S. product, Kraft Macaroni and Cheese Dinner. This radio is 4" H and requires earphones for use. It has a belt clip and is AM/FM. $40-55.

Libby's® Canned Meats radio was made in Hong Kong. It is a can-type radio advertising Libby's other products on the label. $35-50.

LeGoût® Chicken Base and LeGoût Minestrone are AM radios, both made in Hong Kong. The Chicken Base is 4.75" H and the Minestrone is 3.75" H. $30-50 each.

Big Mac cube radio was made in Hong Kong by General Electric and distributed for McDonald's Corp®. It is shaped like a red cube with "Big Mac" printed in yellow letters. It is 4" W and 2.75" H. $35-50.

McDonald's Coast to Coast is a standard, soda-sized can radio. It commemorates McDonald's from 1955-1985. Both sides of the label have a winking hamburger carrying a sign. This radio was made in Hong Kong. $35-60.

McIlhenney® Tabasco Pepper Sauce is an AM/FM radio made in China. It is a can-type radio with the word "Tabasco" printed in red on the front. This radio is 5" H. $50-75.

McDonald's French Fries radios are almost the same, but the one with the antenna pulled up slightly in the box is AM/FM. The radio pictured with no antenna is an AM model. Both radios were made in Hong Kong and measure about 6" H. $45-60 each.

Parkay® Margarine is an AM radio made in Hong Kong. It is 4.5" H and has an attached carrying strap. It looks exactly like a box of margarine. $45-60.

Miracle Whip® Jar is an AM radio made in Hong Kong. It is 5" H with a speaker in the lid and thumbwheels on both sides for volume and tuning. It looks very realistic. $35-60.

Oreo (like) Cookie is dated 1977 and made by Amico. This radio looks like an Oreo cookie with a bite taken out of it, but does not specify what kind of cookie it is. It is 6" W and AM only. $20-40.

Carter's Peanuts is an AM radio made to spoof Jimmy Carter's peanut connections. This radio has a smiling figure on the front. It is plastic with a metal carrying handle. This unit was made in Hong Kong and is 3.5" H. $25-40.

Fisher's® Party Peanuts is a can-type radio. It has thumbwheels on the sides and a speaker on the top. It is the same size as the real product. $25-40.

Pizza Hut® is a pocket-style radio measuring 3.75" H. The radio came with matching headphones in the shape of pizzas. $50-65.

Planter's® Cocktail Peanuts radio has the character "Mr. Peanut" on the label. This unit is a life-sized copy, with the usual speaker on the top of the can. $35-50.

Quaker Quick Oats® has an old style label with a recipe on the back. This AM radio was made in Hong Kong and is smaller than the actual product. It measures 4.75" H. $90-115.

Carolina® Enriched Rice is a box-style AM radio and stands 4.75" H. It was made in Hong Kong. The box is decorated with cooking instructions on the back. $25-40.

Mahatma® and Watermaid® Rice is another AM radio made in Hong Kong. The box is 4.75" H and 3.5" W. The speaker is on the Watermaid side, with a lady figure pictured. The Mahatma side has a man pictured. $30-50.

Success® Rice is an AM radio and was made in Hong Kong. This unit also has the cooking instructions on the back. It measures 4.75" H and 3.5" W. $50-75.

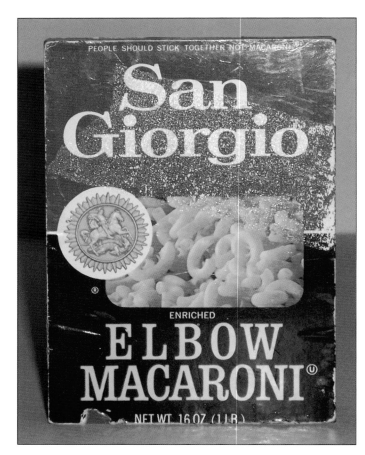

San Giorgio® Elbow Macaroni is an AM radio made in Hong Kong. It also is 4.75" H. This unit has a recipe on the back. $45-60.

Cracker Jack® is a two-sided box radio. One side sits horizontal and the other side sits vertical, advertising the product. This radio is AM and made in Hong Kong. It measures 5" H and 2.75" W. $75-100.

Skinner® Macaroni is a box-style radio and displays its product information on all sides of the box. It stands 5" H and was also made in Hong Kong. $45-60.

Keebler® Animal Crackers is a colorfully printed box radio with a plastic handle on top for carrying. This unit is life-sized. $60-85.

Kit Kat by Nestlé® is an AM/FM box radio with a carrying strap attached. It is dated 1996 and measures 4.5" W and 3" H. 25-40.

Mr. Tom® Peanut Crunch is the size of a real candy bar, easily fitting in a pocket. It is FM only. $15-25.

Little Debbie® is a small, credit card sized radio, only measuring .5" thick, 2.25" H, and 3.5" L. It is AM/FM and requires earphones for use. $20-35.

Nacho n' Corn Thins is a box-style radio, advertising this Nabisco® product on all sides of the box. It is plastic with a paper label. $35-50.

Party Pizza by Totino's® is an AM/FM radio made in Hong Kong. It is 4.75" H and requires one 9 volt battery for operation. $30-50.

Nestlé Crunch is an AM radio with an attached carrying strap. It has blue and red printing. It is 2.25" H and 4" W. $40-50.

Rold Gold® Baked Pretzels is a "wafer-type" radio, so named for its thin build. It is .5" thick and 3" W. This unit needs earphones for use and has a long cord attached for wearing as a necklace. $10-25.

Starburst® is a scanner-type radio, and is a life-sized copy of the candy. It has an attached belt clip and requires earphones for use. $10-25.

Salerno® Butter Cookies is a credit card sized radio made in China. It is FM and requires earphones for use. It measures .5" thick, 3.5" H, and 2.25" W. $25-40.

Trebor® Softmints is an AM/FM radio about the size of a soda can. It stands 4.75" H and the thumbwheels are located on the sides. $35-50.

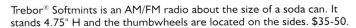

Tic-Tac® radio is much larger than the real product. It is 4" H and has an obvious antenna and light on the top of the box. $20-35.

Weet-Bix® is a pocket-style radio with an attached carrying strap. The red, white, and blue label reads "New Zealand's favourite WHOLE WHEAT malted biscuits." $35-50.

Nestlé Souptime sits 4.75" H. This radio was made in Hong Kong using a common mold, which was used on many of the plastic box radios. $35-50.

Campbell's® Cup 2 Minute Soup Mix is an actual-sized copy of the product. It advertises chicken noodle soup. The thumbwheel is on the left side of the box. $35-50.

Lipton® Cup-a-Soup is a box-style radio made of plastic with a paper label. It has thumbwheels on top for volume and tuning. The label reads "Instant – Just Add Boiling Water." This unit was made in Taiwan. $35-50.

Campbell's Chicken Noodle Soup is an AM/FM can-type radio. This unit was packaged with a coal kit, an actual can of the soup, and a can that dispenses tissues. It is about 4.5" H. $35-50.

Campbell's Tomato Soup #1 is an AM radio. It was made in Hong Kong, with thumbwheels on both sides. This can is not an exact likeness of the can of soup. It stands 4" H. $35-50.

Campbell's Tomato Soup #2 is an AM/FM radio. It is valued about the same, but looks more like the soup can than the previous AM version. It stands 4.5" H. $35-50.

Heinz Tomato Soup is a two-sided radio made in Hong Kong. The thumbwheels are located on both sides of this AM unit. The back of the radio has a woman pictured in the center of the label. It stands 3.5" H. $40-60.

Spam® is an AM radio with an attached carrying strap. It was made in Taiwan and mirrors its product very closely. It stands 3.25" H. $50-75.

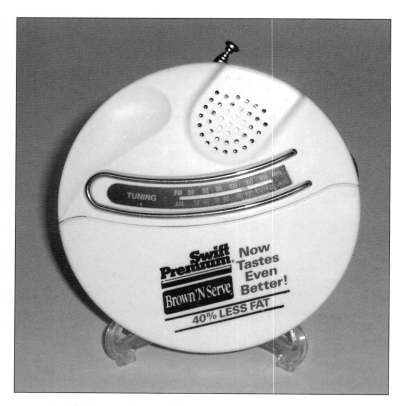

Swift® Premium Brown n' Serve is an AM/FM radio. It must be seated on a stand to display. It is 4.25" H and has an attached belt clip and strap for carrying. $25-40.

Van Camp's® Beanee Weenee is an actual sized copy of the product. It is difficult to spot as a radio, and stands 5" H. This AM/FM radio was made in China. $35-50.

Taco Bell® is a thin, pocket-sized radio. It is 1" thick, 3.5" H, and 2.25" W. This unit is AM/FM and requires earphones for use. It was made in China. $35-60.

Freshlike® Green Beans and Sweet Corn is a two-sided can radio. This AM/FM unit pictures corn on one side and green beans on the other side. The radio is dated 1991 and stands 4" H. $35-50.

Niblets Corn by Green Giant® is an older AM radio. It has the Jolly Green Giant pictured on the label and stands 3.5" H. This radio was made in Taiwan. $40-60.

Lil' Sprout radio is a molded plastic unit and contains trademarks of the Pillsbury® Company. This figure is the Jolly Green Giant's son. The radio was made in Hong Kong and stands 8.25" H. $35-50.

Chapter Six

Soda Pop, Juice, and Other Drink Advertising

7-Up wafer is an AM radio with an attached belt clip on the back. It measures 3.5" across and requires earphones for use. $15-25.

7-Up vending machine is a rare AM/FM radio. It was made in Hong Kong and stands 7" H. $85-115.

A & W® Root Beer float is a large AM/FM radio. It measures 10.5" H and 7.25" L. This unit is mounted on a waterproof lifeboat. The front reads "Music Boat." This radio was made in Hong Kong. $40-65.

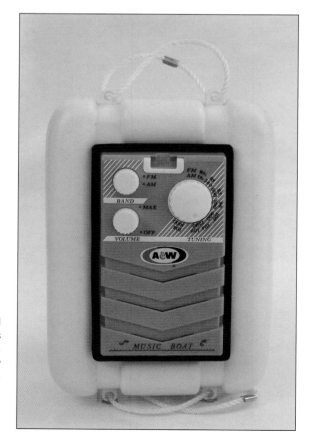

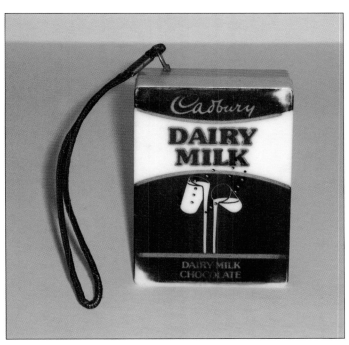

Borden® Milk Shake is a can-type radio with French printing on one side. It is the size of a soda can and was made in Hong Kong. $35-50.

Cadbury Dairy Milk is a pocket-type radio. It is plastic and the print was directly applied to the surface. It has an attached carrying strap. $20-35.

Coca Cola® and Astros is a pocket-type AM radio. It also advertises Kroger on the front. This radio requires earphones for use. $15-25.

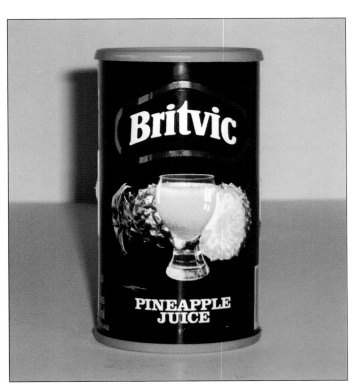

Coca Cola group of bottles shows three different sizes and types of radios. The smallest radio is just over 3" H and the largest is almost 8" H. These radios are pictured individually and detailed next.

Britvic® Pineapple Juice is another soda can sized radio. It has a pineapple and a glass of juice pictured on the front. It has thumbwheels on both sides. $35-50.

Coca Cola mini bottle is the mid-sized bottle of the three pictured earlier. It is small, only 5" H, but not the smallest of that grouping. The cap turns to tune this made in China radio. $20-35.

Coca Cola bottle is the largest of the three bottles previously pictured. It is very life-like in size and shape. It is 7.75" H. If inspected closely, the speaker holes in the front are visible. $20-35.

Coca Cola bottle #1 is one of a series that was produced for foreign distribution. This unit is printed in Japanese. The box is also printed in Japanese. All the bottles in this series are FM, and stand 7.75" H. $35-50.

Coca Cola tiny, mini is the smallest of the group of the three radios. It is only 3.25" H and requires earphones for use. This unit is FM only. $10-25.

Hardee's® Coca Cola bottle is a life-sized copy of the product. It is 7.75" H. Its only difference from the other Coca Cola bottles is the red cap, which identifies it with Hardee's restaurants. This radio was made in Hong Kong. $35-50.

Coca Cola bottle #2 is another foreign radio, printed in Korean. Its characteristics are the same as the previous Japanese bottle. $35-50.

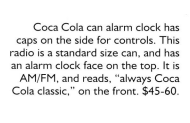

Coca Cola can alarm clock has caps on the side for controls. This radio is a standard size can, and has an alarm clock face on the top. It is AM/FM, and reads, "always Coca Cola classic," on the front. $45-60.

Coca Cola bottle #3 is also in the foreign series. It is printed in Russian. $35-50.

Coca Cola bottle #4 is printed in Thai and is last example of the foreign radios. $35-50.

Coke can has French printing on the front. It is a standard can size and reads "Savourez" above the word "Coke." $20-35.

Diet Coke can #1 has a shiny, grey background. This radio has a glass pictured on the front with bubbles all around the print. It is a standard size can. $20-35.

Coca Cola variety group pictures different containers with various features. These radios are pictured in this chapter.

Diet Coke can #2 is plastic with a white paper label. It has the words "taste Diet Coke" with the Coke wave printed in red on the label. It is a standard size can. $20-35.

Coca Cola Australian mini is a small can-style radio. It is only 3" H and 1.5" W. This radio requires earphones for operation. $25-40.

Coca Cola can with wave is an AM radio. It is a standard size can. The radio is plastic with a paper label. $25-40.

Coca Cola cup with straw has a bottle pictured on the front. It is an AM/FM radio and stands 4.5" H. $25-40.

Large and Small Olympic cans pictures two sizes of the radios commemorating the '92 Barcelona Games.

Large Olympic can is an FM radio. The print on the can has the Olympic rings and it reads "Barcelona '92." The volume control is located on the top of the can, and the tuner is on the bottom. It stands 4.75" H. $45-60.

Small Olympic can is also an FM only radio. It is small, only measuring 3.5" H and 2" W. It reads "Barcelona '92" like the larger can. It must have earphones for operation. $45-60.

Small Coca Cola can has control buttons on the top. It is smaller than a standard can, and requires earphones for operation. This radio is FM only. $10-20.

Coca Cola Toujours is an AM/FM radio. The word "Toujours" and a bottle are printed on the front. It is a standard size can. $45-60.

Coca Cola can with World Wide Olympic Partner script on the label. This radio is a standard size soda can. It is AM/FM. $45-60.

Coca Cola bottle cap is 3.25" across. It was made in China and requires earphones for use. This radio is AM/FM. $15-25.

Coca Cola chest looks like an old style cooler, but is a fairly new radio. It is a weather scanner, has TV bands, and is an AM/FM radio. This unit was made in China and measures 6" W. $35-60.

Coca Cola CKAC pocket radio has the word "Classique" printed at the bottom. It has an attached carrying strap. It has the Coca Cola wave printed across the front with the "CKAC 73 AM" logo decorating the top left corner. $25-40.

Coca Cola fold-up
radio is a scanner-type
model. It contains a
lamp in the top section
and folds down for
easy storage. This radio
was made in Korea.
$20-35.

Coca Cola cube radio is an FM model, 2.75" cubed. It is an off-white
color, with large knobs on the top for volume and tuning. The front of
the cube says "EK DESIGN." This radio was made in China. $25-40.

Coca Cola fold-out radio is an AM/FM radio that has speakers that pull out to make the unit 7" W
when opened. $20-35.

Coca Cola House is a plastic radio
in the shape of a house with a red
brick print on the label. One side
of the house has a picture of a
large bottle across the Coca Cola
logo. It is 3" H and is an FM
scanner. The back of the house
has all the control knobs and jacks
for DC and earphones. $20-35.

Coca Cola mini wafer radio is a thin plastic model. It has a red and black soccer ball print as a background for the Coca Cola logo on the front. This radio requires earphones for use. It measures about 3.5" across. $10-20.

Coca Cola R-A-D-I-O is an AM radio. It is shaped as the letters R,A,D,I,O. The speaker is located in the letter "O" and the Coca Cola logo is clearly printed in red across the letter "I." $60-85.

Coca Cola scanner is a clear, red, plastic radio. It can only be used with earphones and is an FM scanner only. $10-20.

Vanilla Coke is also an FM scanner. It is a clear, red, plastic color and has a flashlight feature. $10-20.

Red Coca Cola T-Shirt is molded in the shape of a shirt. The background color is red with the Coca Cola logo printed in white. It was made in China. This radio is an FM scanner with an attached antenna on the back. It stands 6.25" H. $15-30.

White Coca Cola T-Shirt is the same mold as the red T-shirt. It has a white background with red printing. It was made in China and is also an FM scanner. $15-30.

Coca Cola button radio is about the size of a large button. It has attached earphones and is FM only. It is about 1.5" W. $10-20.

Coca Cola Vending Machine #1 is an AM/FM radio made in Japan. This radio stands 8" H and has 10 bottles appearing vertically on the left side of the front. It looks like it is made of metal and plastic, but is actually all plastic. $85-110.

Coca Cola Vending Machine #4 is an older model, and much more scarce than units #1, #2, and #3. This radio is AM/FM and stands 7.75" H. It was made in Japan and appears to vend bottles. It has a clear plastic cover on the top, front, with a paper label inside. The label reads "Drink Coca-Cola." $150-175.

Coke Vending Machine #2 is also 8" H. This unit was made in Hong Kong and vends several coke products. The word "Coke" is printed vertically on the front. This radio is AM/FM. $85-110.

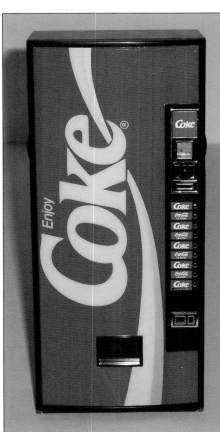

Coke Vending Machine #3 has the Coke logo printed vertically on the front. This unit also has the Coke wave on the front. It stands 7.25" H, and was made in Japan. This radio is AM/FM and is not as valuable as vending machines #1 and #2. $40-60.

Coca Cola Vending Machine #5 is an AM/FM radio made to look like the 1955 model unit. The logo "Neat-O" is printed on the bottom right corner. This radio is the smallest of the vending machines, only 7" H. $65-100.

Cup and Saucer is a molded plastic unit. This radio has a large speaker on the top of the cup, colored brown to look like coffee. It was made in Hong Kong and measures 2.75" H and 5.25" W. $25-40.

Folger's® Coffee is an AM can-type radio. It looks large, but is only 3.5" H. The label reads "Mountain Grown," just like the actual product. This radio was made in Hong Kong and uses one 9 volt battery. $50-75.

Coffee Time® Coffee Cup is molded to look like a large coffee mug with a spoon sticking up inside it. The thumbwheels are visible on the sides of this unit. $25-40.

Hershey's Milk is a button-sized radio. It is an FM receiver and requires earphones for use. $15-25.

Hi-C® Boppin' Berry/ Jammin' Apple is a two-sided radio. It looks like drink box, with Boppin' Berry flavor on one side and Jammin' Apple on the other side. This radio is 5" H and 3" W, with an attached carrying strap. $35-50.

Koolaid® Bursts radios are shaped and sized to match the drink bottles they advertise. They are both 8" H and have attached carrying straps. These radios have twistable tops and bases for tuning, off/on, and volume. They are AM/FM and are dated 1992. $15-25 each.

Justea radio is shaped like a lemon with large legs to stand on. The front of the lemon has green buttons for reset and scan, where a pair of eyes would be. The logo, "Yeo's,"® is also on the front, and an antenna pulls out of the top of the lemon's head. $15-25.

Libby's Pineapple/ Apple Nectar is a two-sided radio. It advertises Pineapple Nectar on one side and Apple Nectar on the other side. This radio is a life-sized can, made in Hong Kong. $35-50.

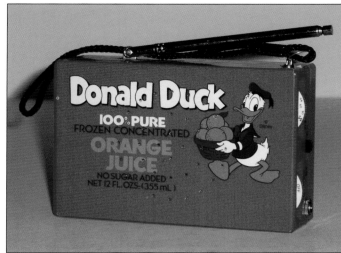

Lipton Tea Cup is shaped like a cup and saucer and advertises "Jiggler Lemon Tea Bags" on the front. It is 3.5" H and is colored yellow to accent the product. This radio was made in Hong Kong. $25-40.

Donald Duck Orange Juice is a box-style radio with an attached carrying strap. It has a picture of Donald Duck on the front and measures 4.5" H and 3" W. This radio is AM/FM. $50-65.

Milk Carton radio is the size of a half-pint container. Its antenna is the straw sticking out of the top. This radio stands 5.5" H to the top of the straw. It is AM/FM. $20-35.

Sunkist® Orange is a box-style radio with the German printing "Fructsaftgetrank mit Traubenzucker-Zusatz" written on both sides of the label. It is AM and stands 3.25" H. $10-25.

Pepsi® bottle #1 is a newer looking version of the soft drink bottle. It is an AM radio made in Hong Kong. This unit is plastic, but looks like a glass bottle, and stands 9.75" H. $20-40.

Pepsi can #2 has a digital clock in the front. This radio is AM/FM and is a standard can size. $25-40.

Pepsi bottle #2 has the older style Pepsi logo on the front. It is smaller than the #1 bottle, only 8.25" H. This unit is also AM. $45-60.

Pepsi can #1 has the logo "Pepsi" printed on a glossy background vertically. This radio is AM/FM and is a life-sized can. $25-40.

Pepsi can #3 is a standard-size soda can. The "Pepsi-Cola" logo is printed in dark blue. There is a wide, lighter blue stripe near the bottom of the can. This AM radio has thumbwheel controls on both sides. $25-40.

Pepsi can #4 advertises "Chart Show Network," a radio show, on the can. This radio is also a life-sized can. $25-40.

Pepsi Free can has the words "Pepsi Free" printed diagonally in blue on a white can. This radio is AM only and is a life-sized can. $25-40.

Diet Pepsi can is printed in red, white, and blue with slashes across the bottom logo. The words "Diet Pepsi, One Calorie" are written on the front. This radio is a life-sized can. $25-40.

Red/Blue Pepsi can is a life-sized AM radio. It's "Pepsi" logo is printed on a flat-colored background. One side of the can has a vertical red stripe down the bottom and the other side of the can has a vertical blue stripe down the bottom. $25-40.

Pepsi Light cans both advertise the product "Pepsi Light," produced for a very short time. One radio has the logo printed in white letters horizontally. The other radio has a white and yellow logo printed diagonally across the front. Both units are AM, made in Hong Kong. $25-40 each.

Pepsi-Cola cap radio is molded in the shape of a large Pepsi bottle cap. This AM/FM radio is 6.5" across. It was made in China. $35-50.

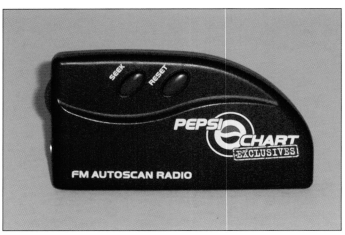

Pepsi Can Scanner is a small radio with earphones attached. It measures 3.5" H and 2" across. This unit is an FM scanner only. $15-25.

Pepsi Chart Scanner radio is only about 2" W. It is an FM scanner, and requires earphones for use. $10-20.

Pepsi Box is a pocket-sized radio. It has no speaker and requires headphones for use. This unit is an AM radio. $15-25.

Pepsi-Cola pocket radio is a common unit, but a really nicely decorated one. The front of this radio has an older-looking Pepsi-Cola bottle cap on the top right corner. There is another bottle cap in the middle of the large speaker on the front. The words "Ice Cold" are printed on the bottom of the front. This AM/FM radio has an attached carrying strap and a large tuner in the front. $25-35.

Pepsi-Cola Vending Machine is a nice looking pocket-sized radio. This unit has the Pepsi-Cola logo in large print in the center. This AM/FM radio also functions as a cassette player. The top left corner has a picture that looks like a coin slot with a price of 10 cents under it. $35-50.

Pepsi Fountain Dispenser looks like an old soda fountain. It reads "Say Pepsi, Please" and has large buttons on the front for controls. This Japanese unit has a molded plastic glass sitting at the bottom of the fountain and comes with a removable leather carrying harness. It is an AM radio and stands 7" H. $200-250.

Pepsi Guitar radio is 13" L, and reads "Ask For More" on the body. It is molded in a very life-like shape of a guitar, including strings. This unit is a scanner only. $25-40.

Pepsi Mini Ball is an FM scanner. It is a small red, white, and blue colored unit with a long cord attached so it can be hung around the neck. $10-20.

Pepsi pocket-sized radio reads "*Indiana Jones and the Last Crusade*" on the front. This radio has a tan and brown background with the red, white, and blue Pepsi logo brightly pictured on it. It is an AM/FM radio requiring earphones. $25-40.

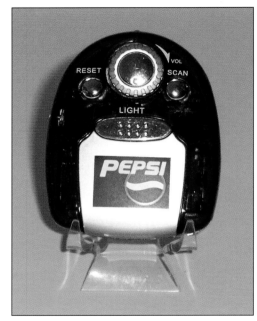

Pepsi Mini Scanner is a radio similar to the earlier Coca Cola scanner. This unit is a transparent blue color with the Pepsi logo printed on it. It must have earphones for use. $10-20.

Pepsi R-A-D-I-O is a colorful red, white, and blue radio. It is molded in the shape of the word "Radio." The speaker is in the center of the "O" and the Pepsi logo is in the middle of the letter "I." $50-75.

Pepsi Junior is a red plastic pocket-sized radio. It stands 5" H. The speaker cover in the front spans almost the entire length of this radio. $20-35.

Pepsi Vending Machine #1 is an AM/FM radio. It vends four different Pepsi products. This unit stands 8" H, and has a visible antenna on the top. $45-60.

Pepsi Vending Machine #2 is also 8" H. This radio vends seven different Pepsi products. Unlike the previous unit, this radio has no visible antenna. $45-60.

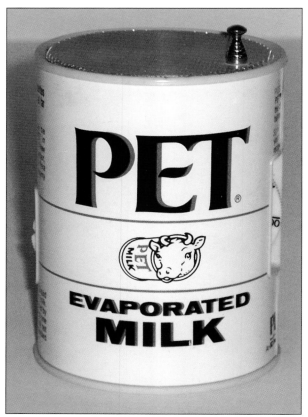

Pet® Evaporated Milk is a can-type radio with a picture of a cow on the label. It was made in Hong Kong and stands 4" H. This unit is AM/FM. $60-80.

Pepsi Vending Machine #3 reads "Say Pepsi Please" on the front. It is an AM radio with a removable leather case. The Pepsi logo has a bottle cap in its background. This unit is 6.75" H and is one of the rarer radios. $150-200.

Pepsi Vending Machine #4 is colored white on top and blue on the bottom. It is an AM/FM radio with an antenna attached in the back. The front reads "Drink Pepsi-Cola The Original Pure Food Drinks!" $35-50.

Punchy is the mascot for Hawaiian Punch® fruit drink. This radio is molded in the shape of "Punchy" and stands 6.5" H. This unit was distributed by R.J. Reynolds® Tobacco via Specialty Advertising Products. It was made in Hong Kong. $50-75.

Robinson's® Orange Juice Drink is advertised on the other side of the Ribena radio. This side has oranges pictured at the bottom with the promise "with whole oranges" written on it. $25-40.

Ribena® Black Currant Juice Drink is a two-sided box-style radio with an attached carrying strap. One side has a nice picture of the purple fruits on the top and the bottom. This radio was produced by Isis® advertising for the British market. $25-40.

Hubba Bubba® is a soda can-sized radio with the words "Original Bubble Gum Soda" printed on the label. It was made in Hong Kong and has thumbwheels on the sides for tuning and volume. $45-60.

Tetley® Round Tea Bags is a small, wafer-type radio. It has an attached cord long enough to wear as a necklace. This radio is only 2" across. $20-35.

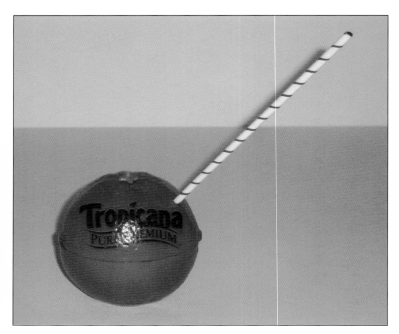

Tropicana® Orange is a molded plastic radio shaped and sized like an orange. There is a 6" long straw sticking out of the orange, which serves as the antenna. This orange-shaped radio is 4" across and AM/FM. This is a fairly common unit, but is frequently found with the straw (antenna) missing. $10-25.

V-8® is a life-sized can radio. It reads "100% vegetable juice" on the front. The entire label has product information on it. The thumbwheels on the sides of the can serve as controls. $30-45.

Welch's® Grape Juice is a can-type radio. It is a life-sized copy of the product, with the exception of the obvious antenna on the top of the can. $35-50.

Vending Machine is an AM/FM radio and stands 7" H. It says "Cold Drinks with ice" on the front, with no particular brand indicated. $60-85.

Yoo-Hoo® Chocolate Flavored Drink is an AM/FM box-style radio. The label is decorated on all four sides, and even has a bar code on it. This radio was made in China, and measures 5" H and 3" W. $45-60.

103

Chapter Seven

Products Around the House Advertising

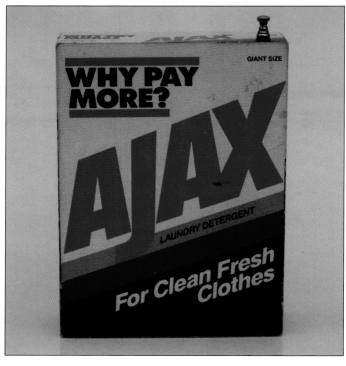

7-11® Cube is an FM receiver radio. The cube is white with the 7-11 logo printed in red and green on the front. It measures 3" on all sides. $20-35.

Ajax pocket radio is an older model, made of plastic with a paper label. It is AM only. It stands 5" H and reads "Why pay more?" on the label. $45-60.

Ajax® 2 is a pocket-sized AM/FM radio. This radio is wrapped in a plastic cover, which has the printing on it. It measures 3.5" W and 4.75" H. $55-70.

Alka-Seltzer® is a plastic radio with an affixed metal cap. It was made in Taiwan and is dated 1971 on the bottom. $55-70.

All® Detergent is a brightly decorated, box-style radio. The print on the front reads "with Bleach, Borax and Brighteners." The back of the box has the directions for use. This radio measures 4.75" H and 3.5" W. $55-80.

Avon Skin-So-Soft is life-sized copy of the product. It was made in China and stands 7.5" H. This AM/FM radio looks so real, it could easily be overlooked as an Avon bottle. $20-35.

Avon® R-A-D-I-O is another molded plastic model in the shape of the word radio. The "O" contains the speaker with the word "Avon" written below it. This radio is 3.5" H and 10" L. $30-50.

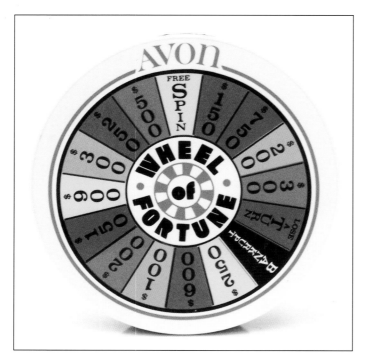

Avon "Wheel Of Fortune" is an FM radio and requires earphones for operation. There is a belt clip attached to the back for easy carrying. This radio is 3.5" across and uses two "AA" batteries. $35-50.

Bon Ami® Polishing Cleanser is a life-sized radio advertising "hasn't scratched yet." The front of the can has a picture of a baby chick, along with the product information. This radio was made in Hong Kong. $45-60.

Avon Zany is another life-sized radio. The bottle stands on one flatted edge, so it looks tilted to one side. This radio was made in Hong Kong, advertising the "Zany" perfume made by Avon. It measures 4.75" H and 5" W. $45-60.

Borax®/Borateem® is a box-type radio advertising two different products. "Borax Detergent" is on one side of the box and "Borateem Bleach" is on the other side. This radio measures 4.75" H and 3.5" W. $60-85.

Marlboro® flashlight radio is an AM/FM unit with a working flashlight. It has an attached belt clip and stands 6.25" H. $10-20.

Winston® flashlight is also an AM/FM radio with a working flashlight. It has a carrying strap instead of a belt clip. This unit is also 6.25" H. $10-20.

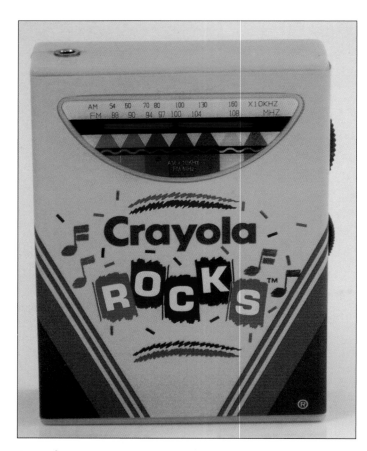

Glad® Sandwich Bags is a pocket-sized radio. It is plastic with a paper label. The print has a yellow background with musical notes surrounding the logo. $25-40.

Crayola® Rocks is a mail order product, offered by the company. It was made in China and requires earphones for use. This AM/FM radio looks like a box of crayons, with music notes decorating the front. $35-50.

Halite® is a pocket-sized weather radio with an attached carrying strap. There is a box near the top of the label with the radio station "AKZO" advertised. The product is an ice melting crystal, so it makes sense for this to be used as a weather radio. It was made in China and stands 4.25" H. $35-50.

Dirt Devil is an AM/FM radio. It is red and black with "Dirt Devil by Royal"® printed in white. This radio requires earphones for use. $15-25.

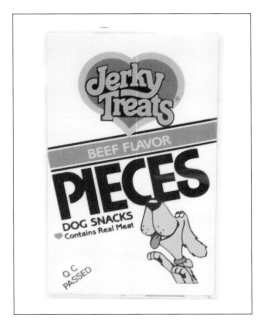

Jerky Treats® is a credit card style radio. It is very thin, and measures 3.25" H and 2" W. It requires earphones for use. There is a picture of a cute dog on the front. $20-35.

John Deere® is an AM/FM pocket-sized radio. The top left corner shows a picture of a deer, with the words "John Deere" written under it. This radio has sliding controls on the front. $25-40.

Kleenex® is a pocket-sized radio with an attached carrying strap. It reads "Kleenex pocket pack" on the front of the paper label. Thumbwheels control the volume and tuning. $25-40.

Kodacolor 400 looks like an actual roll of film. It is 9" L and is decorated on all sides. The front reads "Kodacolor film for color prints" with the Kodak® logo in red print. $25-40.

Joe Camel® on card is an FM radio; it was given away free with a purchase. It is a common radio and requires earphones for use. $10-25.

Kodak Copier is molded in the shape of a copy machine. The front has a label that reads "Kodak Ektaprint Finisher." The Kodak logo is in the center of the radio, printed in red. This unit was made in Hong Kong and measures 6.25" W and 3.5" H. $85-120.

Kodak Instant Color Film is another box radio shaped like a package of film. The label reads "Improved Faster Developing." This Hong Kong radio is 4" square and has an attached carrying strap. $25-40.

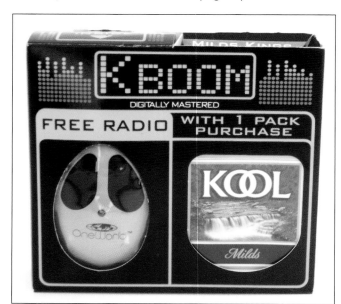

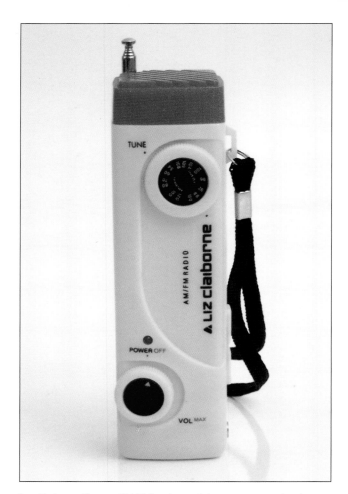

Liz Claiborne® is an AM/FM radio with large tuning and volume dials on the front. It has an attached carrying strap and stands 6.25" H. $15-25.

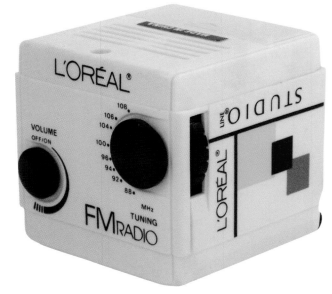

Kool® Cigarettes radio was a promotional give-away with a purchase. The box reads "K Boom" with product information. The radio requires headphones for use. $15-25.

L'Oreal® is an FM radio in a cube shape, 3" on all sides. It was made in China and has large black tuning and volume controls. $30-55.

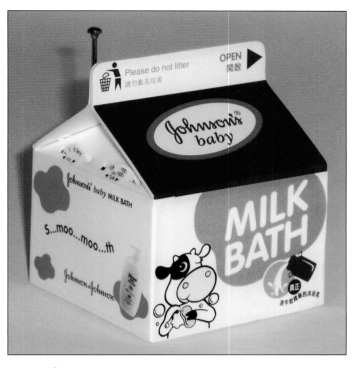

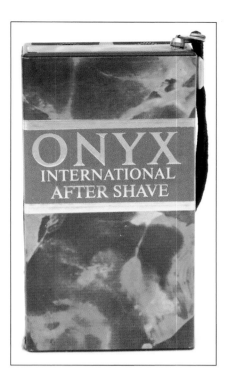

Onyx International® Aftershave is a pocket-style AM radio. The thumbwheel controls are on the top of the radio and it has an attached carrying strap. $35-50.

Johnson's® Baby Milk Bath is shaped like a milk carton with an antenna sticking out of it. This radio is 3.5" H and is AM/FM. The top of the carton has a figure throwing away trash with the writing "Please Do Not Litter." $35-50.

Noxzema® is a box radio and stands 5" H. The paper label reads "Tune Into Noxzema" and has a picture of the product. $35-60.

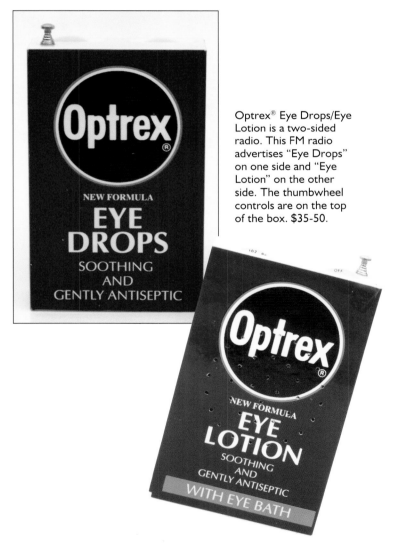

Optrex® Eye Drops/Eye Lotion is a two-sided radio. This FM radio advertises "Eye Drops" on one side and "Eye Lotion" on the other side. The thumbwheel controls are on the top of the box. $35-50.

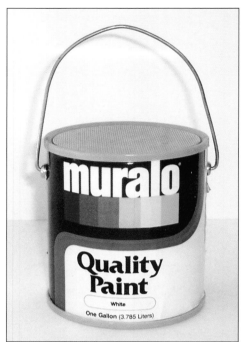

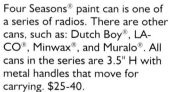

Four Seasons® paint can is one of a series of radios. There are other cans, such as: Dutch Boy®, LA-CO®, Minwax®, and Muralo®. All cans in the series are 3.5" H with metal handles that move for carrying. $25-40.

Pratt & Lambert® paint can is bigger than the other radios. It stands 4" H, and also has a metal handle. $25-40.

Poloroid® 600 Film is an actual-size copy of the product. The radio has a built-in battery pack to power itself. It measures 5" H and 4" W. This radio was made in China. $15-40.

Rugby® Vitamins is an AM/FM can-type radio. The antenna pulls up from the top, and the label reads "minerals supplements" on the front. $35-50.

Purex® Detergent is a box-type radio with a nicely decorated paper label. The box has a blue waterfall in the background with the promise "Super Value!" written on the front. $50-75.

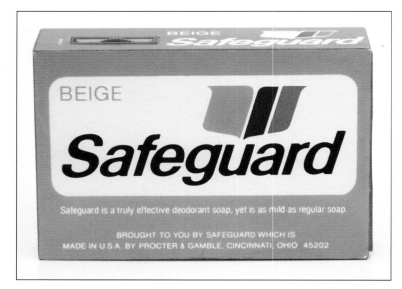

Safeguard® is an AM radio that measures the actual size of the soap. It is 3.5" L and 2.5" H. The box says "Safeguard is a truly effective deodorant soap, yet as mild as regular soap." This radio was made in Hong Kong. $35-50.

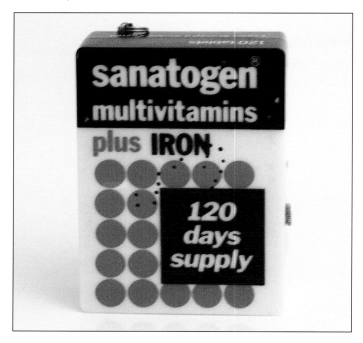

Sanatogen® Multivitamins is a pocket-style radio with an attached carrying strap. The black and red label is printed on its white plastic mold. $25-40.

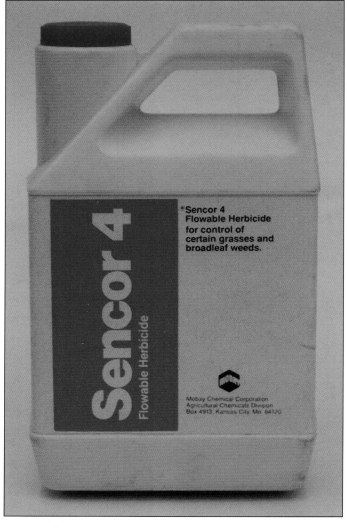

Sencore 4® is shaped like the actual container of the herbicide product. The radio is smaller than life, only 6" H. It was made in Hong Kong, and states "product of Mobay Chemical Corporation." $45-60.

Schick® Quattro is a scanner-type radio made in the mold of a razor's case. The scan and reset buttons are on the front, and a thumbwheel is on one side. $10-25.

Surf® Detergent is an AM/FM radio made in Hong Kong by Isis. It is a pocket-style radio and stands 6.25" H. $60-85.

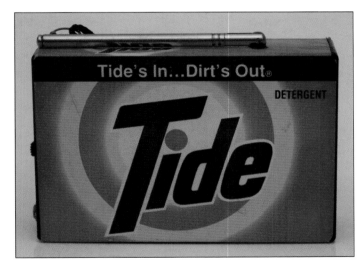

Tide® Detergent is an AM/FM radio with an attached carrying strap. The bottom of the radio gives information about NASCAR racing. The box measures 3" H and 4.25" L. $45-60.

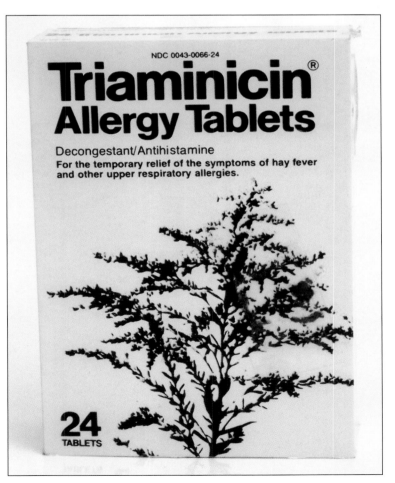

Triaminicin® Allergy Tablets has a nicely decorated label, with dosage information printed on the back. This box-style radio measures 4.75" H and 3.5" W and is dated 1977. $35-60.

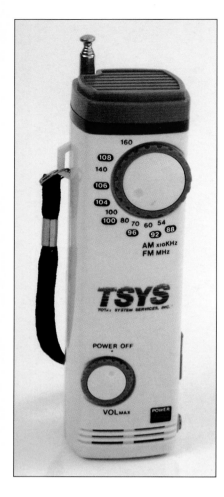

TSYS is an AM/FM radio with a handy carrying strap attached. The front reads "Total Systems Services, Inc."® under the "TSYS" initials. $20-35.

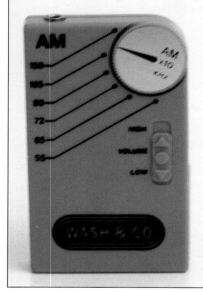

Wash & Go is an AM radio. It has a light blue colored background with darker blue printing. The volume control on the front has only a high and low setting. This radio was made to advertise the Vidal Sasoon® product "Wash & Go." $15-30.

Whiskas® cat food is a can-type radio with a large orange cat on the front. The words "met kip en lever" are printed over the cat's head. $35-50.

Zwitsal® Baby Shampoo is an AM radio shaped and sized to match the product. There is a simple looking picture of a baby on the front, along with two large control knobs. This radio is 8" H and has an attached carrying strap. $45-60.

Chapter Eight

Beer and Liquor Advertising

Anchor® beer #1 is an actual-size FM can radio. The label is colored using a flat white background with red and black printing. $25-40.

Anchor beer #2 is also an actual-size FM can radio. The label on this can has a shiny, silver background with red and black printing. $25-40.

Billy Beer® is an AM radio representing a beer made for the former president's brother, Billy Carter. Billy endorses the beer label with "I had this beer brewed up just for me. I think it's the best I've ever tasted. And I've tasted a lot. I think you'll like it too." $75-100.

Brand Bier® is an actual-size can radio. It is AM/FM. The label says "HET BIER WAAR LIMBURG TROTS OP IS." $25-45.

Budweiser® #1 is an AM radio and measures the same size as an actual can. The label reads "The Largest-Selling Beer In The World" and "The King Of Beers." $25-40.

Budweiser #3 is an AM/FM radio. This label says "Lager Beer." The radio has an antenna on the top and an attached carrying strap. $25-40.

Budweiser #2 is also an AM radio. The printing on the can is all in Hebrew and includes the logos and decorations for the company. $65-80.

Budweiser #4 is another life-sized can radio. The printing on the label reads "Budweiser, King Of Beers" vertically. $25-40.

118

Carlsberg® Beer can was made in Hong Kong. The label says "Copenhagen Denmark, Imported." $25-50.

Castle® Lager is an FM can-type radio. The label has a picture of a castle. $25-40.

Colt 45® is an AM can-type radio. There is a bull on the label with the words "Malt Liquor." $25-40.

Coors® #1 is an AM can-type radio. The label has a shiny silver background with the words "America's Fine Light Beer." $25-40.

Coors #2 is an AM/FM can-type radio. The label is the same as the AM version, but there is an obvious antenna on the top of this can. $25-40.

Encore® is an AM can-type radio. The label reads "1849, Brewmaster's Private Recipe Beer." $25-40.

Foster's® Lager is an AM can-type radio. The label has a large red "F" printed in the center. $45-60.

Grain Belt® is a standard-sized beer can. The background is a shiny silver color. The label reads "From Perfect Brewing Water." $25-40.

Fiji® is an AM can-type radio. The label has bright green and red printing with the word "Bitter" in the center. $35-50.

Guinness®, Malaysia, is an AM can-type radio. The label says "Malaysia BHD." This radio has a black background with the word "Guinness" printed in red. $45-60.

Gilley's® is a standard-sized beer can. This radio has a picture of Micky Gilley inside the state of Texas on the label. The can says "A Premium Texas Beer." This radio is very collectible. $150-180.

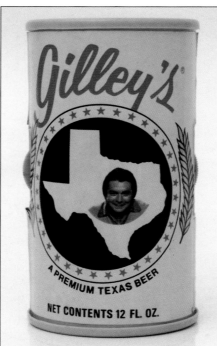

Hamm's® Beer is an AM can-type radio. The label says "America's Classic Premium Beer." $35-50.

Heineken #2 is also a standard can-sized radio. Like the previous can, it was made in Hong Kong and is AM. The label has a red stripe around the top and bottom. $40-55.

Heineken® #1 is a standard can-sized radio. It is AM, made in Hong Kong. The label has a silver background with "Heineken" printed in the center. $35-50.

J R Ewing® is an AM can-type radio. The label says "If you have to ask how much my beer costs, you probably can't afford it." It is signed "J R Ewing." $150-180.

Labatt® 50 *Bière* is an AM can-type radio. The label has two silver coins in the center. $25-40.

Kirin Ichiban® is an FM can-type radio. The label has a dragon on it and is printed in Japanese and English. $50-65.

Labatt's 500/Labatt's Strong is a two-sided AM/FM can. The can has wide gold stripes around the top and bottom. The Labatt's 500 side has a red leaf in the background. $30-45.

Lite Beer® is an AM can-type radio. The label says "A fine pilsner beer." $35-50.

Miller High Life #1 is an AM can-type radio. The label has a shiny gold background with "Miller" and "The champagne of beers" printed in red. $25-35.

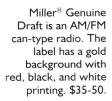

Miller® Genuine Draft is an AM/FM can-type radio. The label has a gold background with red, black, and white printing. $35-50.

Miller High Life #2 is an AM/FM can-type radio. The label on this can is also shiny gold with red print. There is a thin green stripe around the top and bottom of this radio. $20-35.

Modelo® is an AM/FM can-type radio. The words "*Especial Cerveza*" are printed on the label. This radio was made in China. $50-80.

Molson® Expert is an AM can-type radio. The label says "*Bière Ale*" and there is a picture of a ship in the center. $35-50.

O'Keefe® Ale is a standard-sized can radio. The label is printed in French, and says, "*Bière*." There is a knight in armor on the label. $50-80.

Old Style is an AM can-type radio. The background on the label has drawings of a castle, a knight, and other scenery. The radio says "Heileman's"® and "Made with pure, sparkling water." $50-80.

New Castle® Brown Ale is an AM can radio. It stands only 4" H, smaller than an average beer can. This radio was made in Hong Kong. $50-80.

Olympia® Beer is an AM can-type radio. The label has a picture of a horseshoe and the words "It's the water" and "Tumwater." $40-60.

Pearl® Beer is an AM can-type radio. The label says "Fine Lager Beer." $45-60.

Pabst® Blue Ribbon is an AM can-type radio. The label is red, white, and blue with a large blue ribbon on the front. $30-45.

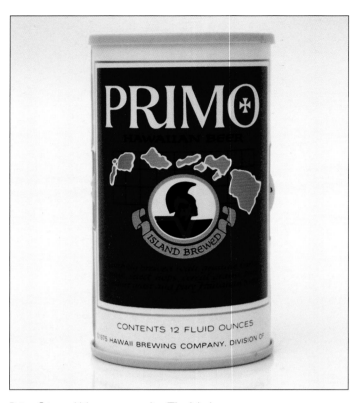

Primo® is an AM can-type radio. The label says "Hawaiian Beer" and "Island Brewed." $45-60.

San Miguel Beer is an AM can-type radio. It was made in Hong Kong. The label says "San Miguel Brewery Limited® Hong Kong." $40-60.

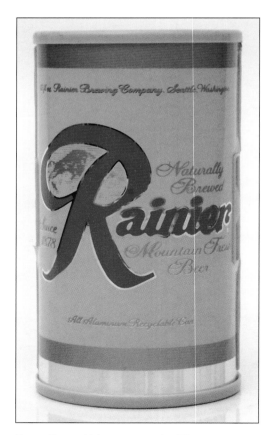

Rainier® is an AM can-type radio. The name of the beer, "Rainier," is printed in large red letters on the label. The remainder of the print is gold-colored. $30-45.

Schlitz® is a standard-sized can radio. The label reads "The beer that made Milwaukee famous." $30-45.

Stroh's #2 is an AM standard-sized can radio. The label says "Bohemian Style Beer" and has a glossy background. This beer can pictures a crown and shield with a lion in the center of it. $25-40.

Schmidt® Beer is a standard-sized can radio. It was made in Hong Kong. The label has a picture of a man ice-fishing. $45-60.

Tecate Cerveza® is an AM can-type radio. The label reads "Hecho en Mexico" at the bottom. It has a red background with black and gold printing. $40-60.

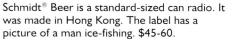

Tres Equis® is an AM can-type radio. The label says "Cerveza Clara" and has a picture of a gold eagle with "XXX" marked in the middle of it in red print. $35-50.

Stroh's® #1 is an AM/FM standard-sized can radio. The label has a flat black background with the word "Stroh's" printed in gold. The remaining print is red and gold. $30-45.

Schlitz Cube is an AM radio made in Japan. It is 3.25" on all sides. There is a large tuning wheel on the top of the cube, with the word "Sony"® printed on it. The Schlitz logo is on the front side. $25-45.

Schlitz Keg is made with the same mold as the Anheiser Keg radio. The metal plate above the spigot reads "Schlitz." The spigot controls the volume on this radio. $75-100.

Budweiser/Bud Light is a pocket-style AM radio. It is a two-sided radio with the word "Budweiser" printed in red on one side. The words "Bud Light" are printed in blue on the other side. The radio also advertises "Baron's" on both sides. It is 3.5" H. $20-35.

Anheiser Keg is a molded plastic radio in the shape of a beer keg. The spigot on the keg controls the volume. There is a metal plate on the front inscribed with "Anheiser Busch, Inc."® The radio measures 6.75" L and 5" in diameter. $75-100.

Cognac Cannon is an AM radio made in Japan. It is made in the shape of a cannon sitting on a base. The bottle reads "Courvoisier"® in red print. The base of the cannon measures 7.25" L. $85-100.

Ballantine's® is a plastic radio with a metal cap and paper labels. The cap functions as a control. The radio measures 8.75" H and was made in Hong Kong. The label reads "Finest Blended Scotch Whisky." $75-100.

Budweiser Bottle looks like an actual beer bottle. It measures 9.5" H and was made in Hong Kong. The radio is plastic with a metal cap and paper labels. $25-40.

The Club® Screwdriver looks exactly like the drink product. This radio came with a built-in shaker and an attached carrying strap. $75-100.

Camus® Grand V.S.O.P. is molded in the shape of a liquor bottle. It stands 10.75" H and was made in Hong Kong. There are two seals on the front of the bottle, which serve as controls. $40-60.

Gold Stripe Canadian Whisky is a can-type radio. The label reads "Thomas Adams Distillery LTD.® Canada." The radio has a black background with a diagonal gold stripe in the center. $30-50.

Flask is an AM radio made in Japan. The body of the flask is black; the top and bottom are a shiny silver color. The cap controls the tuning. The radio measures 4.75" H and 4" W. $45-60.

Grand Old Parr is a molded plastic radio shaped like a liquor bottle. It was made in Japan and stands 5.5" H. The neck of the bottle contains the tuner. The label reads "DeLuxe Scotch Whisky."® 45-60.

Fleischmann's® Gin is a clear plastic radio. It stands 11" H and has paper labels covering it. The "insides" of the radio can be clearly seen. $60-85.

Grolsch® Stopper is a scanner-type radio. It is made in the shape of a bottle stopper. The control buttons are on the front of the radio and it has an attached carrying strap. $20-30.

Old Crow® is an unusual 8 transistor radio. It is molded in the shape of a crow. The penguin is wearing a tuxedo, a hat, and a monocle. He has a cane on his left side, which controls the volume on this radio. The crow is standing on a pedestal that reads "Old Crow" on the front. The back of the pedestal says "Kentucky Whiskies The Old Crow Distillery Co. Frankfort, KY." This radio was made in Japan, and stands 12" H. $350-550.

Pinch® Scotch is a molded plastic radio shaped like the word pinch. The letter "I" contains a bottle with the scotch's information on it. The speaker is in the middle of the letter "C." This radio was made in Hong Kong and measures 2.75" H and 7.5" L. $75-95.

Paul Masson® is shaped like a wine carafe. It was made in Hong Kong and measures 7" H and 3.5" W. The label on the front says "Rare Premium California Burgundy." This radio has thumbwheel controls on both sides and a speaker in the lid. $40-60.

Piper® Brut Champagne is made in the shape of a bottle, complete with paper labels. This radio is 10.5" H and was made in Japan. The labels have French printing on them. $50-70.

Scotch Seven® is another radio shaped like a whisky bottle. It was made in Japan and measures 4.5" H and 1.5" W. This unit is a "transistor micro radio." $45-65.

Seagram's® 7 Wafer is an AM/FM radio. It is 4.25" across and only 1" thick. This radio must have a stand to display it. $35-50.

Canadian Club® Safe was made in Hong Kong. This radio looks like a room safe with moving wheels. The front of the safe is decorated with the print "Canadian Club." This radio is also a bank. $50-75.

Seagram's Benchmark Bourbon is an AM radio shaped like a bottle. It was made in Japan and stands 10" H. The bottle is colored brown so it looks like it contains bourbon. $60-75.

Teacher's® Scotch Whisky is a bottle-shaped radio made in Japan. The cap has volume and tuning controls. $75-90.

Seagram's Cooler is a can-type radio. It is a glossy green color with red printing that reads "Seagram's" and "The Naturally Flavored Citrus And Wine Beverage." $25-40.

Yago's® Sant Gria is a bottle-shaped radio made in Hong Kong. It stands 10.5" H. The bottle is colored to look like it contains liquid. The volume control is in the cap and the tuning is on the bottom. $50-75.

Suntory® Whisky is a bottle-shaped radio with paper labels. The front label reads "Finest Old Liqueur" and "Product of Japan." This radio measures 5" H and 3.25" W. $60-85.

Chapter Nine

Character and Figural

Batman is a two-dimensional AM radio. It was made in Hong Kong. This radio is dated 1978 and has an attached carrying strap. It is 5.5" H. $85-120.

Betty Boop is an AM/FM radio and a digital clock. The Betty Boop figure wears a hat and is sitting on a motorcycle. This radio is 10" H. $45-60.

Benji is an AM radio made in Hong Kong. The Benji figure sits on a blue base with the name "Benji" printed on it. This radio is 6.5" H. $45-60.

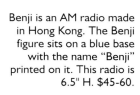

Bugs Bunny is an AM radio. Bugs holds a carrot in one hand and is sitting on a green mound that looks like grass. This radio has an orange carrying strap and is 7" H. It was made in Hong Kong. $25-40.

California Raisin® #1 is an AM radio with posable arms and legs. It was made in China and stands 7" H. The raisin figure is holding a microphone. $35-60.

Charlie The Tuna bike radio has a clamp attached that fastens to a bike's handlebars. It was made in Hong Kong and measures 3.25" W and 5.25" H. The radio has a raised image of "Charlie" under water with a sign that says "Sorry Charlie." $50-75.

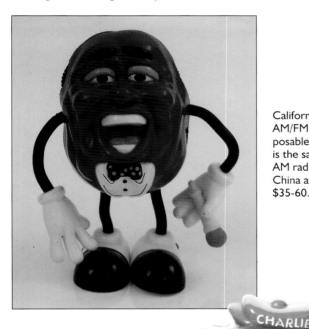

California Raisin #2 is an AM/FM radio with posable arms and legs. It is the same mold as the AM radio. It was made in China and stands 7" H. $35-60.

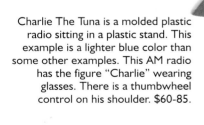

Charlie The Tuna is a molded plastic radio sitting in a plastic stand. This example is a lighter blue color than some other examples. This AM radio has the figure "Charlie" wearing glasses. There is a thumbwheel control on his shoulder. $60-85.

Dudley Do-Right is a cube-shaped radio made in Hong Kong. There is an image of "Dudley" on one side of the cube, showing him on a rocking horse. The cube sits on a base that allows it to turn to view all four images. This radio is 3.75" square. $20-35.

Dukes Of Hazzard is a two-dimensional radio with images of the "Duke" brothers and their car on the front. It was made in Hong Kong and measures 7.5" L and 4.25" W. This radio is dated 1981. $25-60.

Elvis is an AM radio with a sparkly dressed "Elvis Presley" figure standing on a pedestal. He is holding a microphone. The radio is plastic, but the jumpsuit worn by the figure is made of cloth. This radio is 9.5" H and was made in Hong Kong. $45-70.

The Fonz is made in the shape of a jukebox with a picture of Henry Winkler (The Fonz) inside. This radio was made in Hong Kong and measures 6" H and 4.5" W. "Happy Days" is printed on the side and "The Fonz" is printed on the front. The radio is dated 1977. $35-60.

Garfield is a small AM/FM radio. It is only 3" H and requires earphones for use. It is molded in the shape of Garfield's head. There is an attached belt clip on the back. $15-25.

Golly radio is a wafer-type FM radio. It is 3" W and has a long cord attached for wearing as a necklace. There is a dancing figure pictured on the front. This radio requires earphones for use. $15-25.

Garfield with Odie Charm is an AM radio made in Hong Kong. It has an attached plastic charm with an Odie figure on it. This radio is 3.5" W. $45-60.

Ghostbusters is an FM radio made in China. It says "The real Ghostbusters" on the front. There is a raised ghost figure in the center of the front. This radio is 4" square. $20-35.

The Grinch is an AM/FM radio molded in the shape of "The Grinch" wearing sunglasses. The speaker is located in the top lip, making it look like whiskers. It stands 9" H and was made in China. $20-35.

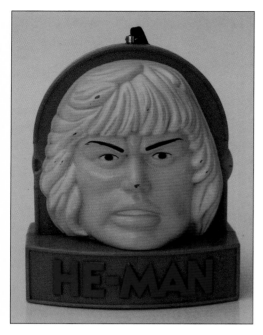

He-Man/Skeletor is a two-sided radio made in Hong Kong. One side has "He-Man" in the center and the other side has "Skeletor" inside it. This radio is dated 1984 and measures 5" H and 4" W. $30-50.

John Wayne is an AM radio and stands 11.5" H. The figure is wearing a cloth western outfit with a hat. He stands on a pedestal that says "John Wayne The Duke May 1907-June 1979." This radio was made in Hong Kong. $75-100.

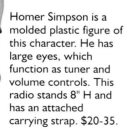

Homer Simpson is a molded plastic figure of this character. He has large eyes, which function as tuner and volume controls. This radio stands 8" H and has an attached carrying strap. $20-35.

Kiss is an FM scanner radio made in China. It is still in the package with earphones included. This radio measures 3" across and must have earphones to operate. $15-25.

M&M® Blue Wafer is an FM radio. It is round with a winking face. The strap has an antenna built-in and there is a belt-clip attached to the back. This radio is 3.5" across. $25-40.

M&M with Headphones is a standing blue figure wearing sunglasses. These were made in many different colors. This radio was made in China, and stands 5" H. $15-25.

M&M Green Wafer is an FM radio. This example is still in the package. The antenna is built into the strap. The radio pictures an orange M&M dancing and a blue M&M that functions as a tuner. There is candy inside the package with the radio. $25-40.

M&M Scuba is a sitting red figure dressed in scuba gear. The spear he is holding is the antenna. This radio is AM/FM and is 4.75" H. It was made in many other colors. $15-30.

M&M with Microphone is a standing blue figure on a yellow base. This radio is motion-activated. It is AM/FM and was made in China. This radio is 10.5" H. $45-60.

M&M Mini is a red figure, with white arms and legs, standing. It is an AM/FM radio with an attached belt-clip. This radio is only 4.5" H. $15-30.

Mickey Mouse in Car is a molded plastic radio made in the shape of the character in a red car. There is a yellow tuning wheel under the driver's side of the car and Mickey appears to be looking up. It measures 4.25" H and 6.25" L. This radio was made in Hong Kong. $75-100.

M&M with Umbrella is a standing yellow figure holding a clear umbrella. The top of the umbrella has an attached carrying strap. This AM/FM radio was made in China and stands 10.5" H. $35-50.

Mickey Mouse is a two-dimensional radio with the words "Mickey Mouse 2 Transistor" printed at the bottom. Mickey has large black ears that contain the tuner and volume controls. $50-75.

Mickey Mouse Head is a two-dimensional radio made in Hong Kong. This figure is wearing a blue shirt. There is a carrying strap attached and a thumbwheel on the top of the head. This radio measures 6.75" H and 6.5" W. $15-35.

Power Rangers is shaped like a red helmet. It is sitting on a green base. This radio is also a clock. It stands 6.5" H and has thumbwheel controls on the back. $25-50.

Raggedy Ann Toothbrush Holder is a molded plastic radio. It has a plastic figure of Raggedy Ann, a sink, and a toothbrush standing on a white base. The base contains the AM radio. It measures 8" H and 6.25" L and was made in Hong Kong. $45-60.

Raid® Bug is an AM/FM radio with a digital clock. It was made in Hong Kong and measures 7" H and 7" W. There is a large yellow bug leaning on the radio dial. The dial has the word "Raid" printed at the bottom. The bug and the dial are sitting on a red base that contains the knob and button controls. $150-250.

Raggedy Ann and Andy is a two-dimensional radio shaped like a heart. There are Raggedy Ann and Andy figures pictured on the front. It has a long, red, attached carrying strap. The radio is still in its box and is dated 1974. It was made in Hong Kong and measures 4.75" W. $25-40.

Snoopy and Woodstock Milk Carton is an AM/FM radio shaped like a milk carton. The carton has a straw sticking out of it, which serves as an antenna. Snoopy and Woodstock are both pictured on the carton. This radio is 5.5" H, including the antenna. $25-45.

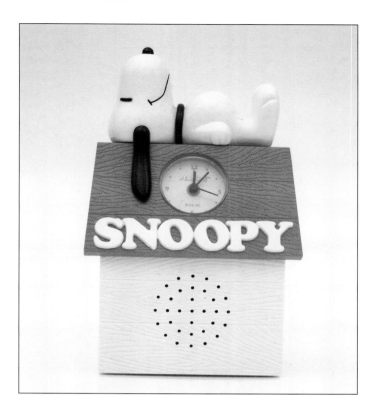

Snoopy on Doghouse is an AM/FM radio with a clock. Snoopy is lying on top of his doghouse. The red roof of the doghouse has the word "Snoopy" printed on it in white letters. The roof also contains the clock dial. This radio stands 7" H. $45-60.

Snoopy on Mound is an AM radio made in Hong Kong. Snoopy is sitting on a green base that appears to be a mound of grass. This radio measures 7" H. $35-50.

Snoopy Jukebox is a molded plastic radio. Snoopy is holding a microphone and has a jukebox attached in front of his stomach. This radio stands 8" H. $45-60.

Snoopy Paint Can is an AM/FM radio. It is made in the shape of a paint can with a metal bail handle. The figure "Snoopy" is pictured on the can wearing a soccer uniform and is kicking a soccer ball. This radio is 3" H. $25-45.

Spiderman Wafer is a thin, round radio made in Hong Kong. It is red with a pair of eyes inside a spider web on the front. It has an attached carrying strap and is dated 1984. This radio is 5" across. $30-50.

Spiderman Head is a molded plastic radio made in Hong Kong. It is red and looks like a mask with only a pair of eyes showing. There are thumbwheel controls at the bottom of the head. This radio was distributed by Amico and is dated 1978. It stands 5" H. $50-75

Sponge Bob Shower is an AM/FM radio. The "Sponge Bob" figure appears to be peeking above a shower curtain. There are knobs on both sides of the radio that function as controls. The shower curtain can be lifted. This radio is 7.5" H. $20-35.

Superman Phone Booth is a molded plastic radio made in Hong Kong. Superman appears to be stepping out of the phone booth, dressed in his superhero outfit. This radio is dated 1978 and measures 7" H and 3" W. $100-175.

Super Mario is a two-dimensional (2-D) AM/FM radio. It is dated 1989 and has an attached carrying strap. This radio measures 5" H and 3.5" W. $10-20.

Superman 2-D is made in the shape of the superhero clenching both fists. There is an attached carrying strap on the top of his head. This radio is dated 1973 and measures 5" W. It was made in Hong Kong. $50-80.

Chapter Ten

Everything Else

@ Symbol is an FM radio made in China. It is molded in the shape of the @ symbol. This radio is 3.5" across. The controls are located on the back. $10-25.

AC Powered Noah's Ark is a table-top radio. The image on the front shows two smiling hippos and lions, with an ark in the background. The radio has a pink background color. It must be plugged into a wall outlet to operate. This radio is 8" H and 8" W. $30-55.

AC Powered Cowboys is a table-top radio. The image on the front shows cowboys jumping over a fence, trying to lasso the moon. The background color is brown. When the radio is plugged in, the image lights up. This mold was used for a large series of other radios with different pictures on them. It measures 8" H and 8" W. $30-55.

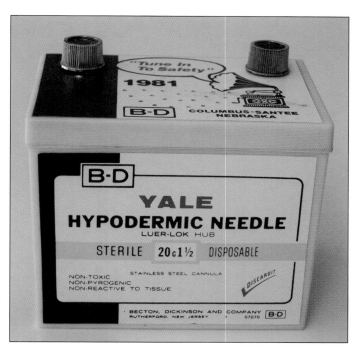

Yale® Hypodermic Needle is an AM radio advertising the product on all sides of the box. The front has information about hypodermic needle disposal. There are two large knobs on the top, which function as controls. The top has a message that reads "Tune Into Safety" and the date "1981." This radio was made in Hong Kong and stands 4" H. $35-50.

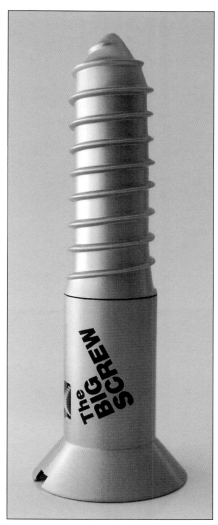

The Big Screw is an AM radio shaped like a large screw. The head of the screw is the tuner. The box is not pictured, but reads "Reasons you deserve The Big Screw" with a long list of reasons. The radio is 8.5" L. $50-75.

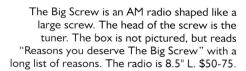

Beanbag is an AM radio shaped like a beanbag. The radio has a large tuning dial on the top and a cloth beanbag attached to the bottom. It was made in Japan and measures 4" across. $35-50.

Butterflies is an AM radio with metal butterflies attached to a plastic green base. The colorful butterflies are suspended above the base with thin wires, making them seem to be in the air. This radio stands 7.5" H. $30-55.

Ditto Man is an AM/FM radio made in China. It is shaped like a man sitting behind a desk. There is a tag on the front that reads "Ditto Man." The man's mouth moves when this radio is played. The radio measures 5" H and 5" W. $30-45.

Crown Royal® London is an AM radio made in Hong Kong. The radio is shaped like a crown, complete with jewels. The outside frame of the crown is plastic and the inside has a red cloth cover. There is a plastic tag attached to the top that reads "Royal London International Collection." There are two large black knobs on the front for tuning and volume. $45-60.

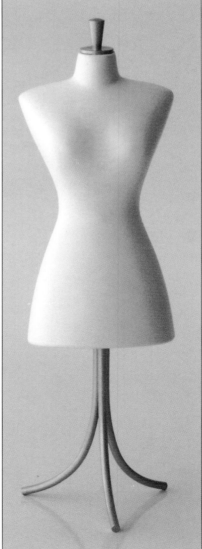

Dress Form is an FM radio shaped like a dress form on a stand. This radio stands 8.5" H. $20-35.

Dancing Bean is an AM radio that looks like a child's toy. It is shaped like a bug with wings and antennae. The stomach has a clear plastic cover that contains beans that will jump when the radio is played. This radio is 5.5" H. $35-50.

Happy Birthday Medallion is a colorful radio with a long chain attached, so it can be worn as a necklace. The speaker holes cover the front of the radio. It is decorated with "Happy Birthday" and numbers in the center. $20-35.

Hippy Flower Girl is a plastic can-type radio. The paper label is brightly decorated with flowers and a lady is pictured holding a handbag. The label reads "Keep America Beautiful!" $25-40.

Jump Rope is an FM radio shaped like a jump rope. It is pictured in its package, which reads "Real FM Radio In The Grip." This is a fairly new radio. $20-30.

149

Kinney® Country is a plastic can-type radio. The paper label has a western background and reads "Opportunity Everywhere." $25-35.

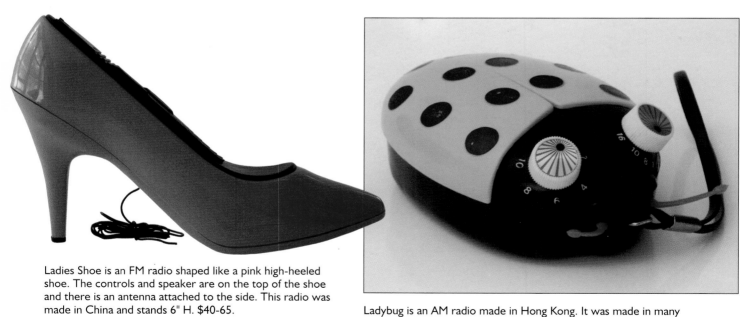

Ladies Shoe is an FM radio shaped like a pink high-heeled shoe. The controls and speaker are on the top of the shoe and there is an antenna attached to the side. This radio was made in China and stands 6" H. $40-65.

Ladybug is an AM radio made in Hong Kong. It was made in many different colors. This radio is the rarest color: yellow, with blue spots. The wings open as the volume is increased and the eyes function as control knobs. The ladybug has plastic red antennae that are very thin and easily broken. This radio measures 1.75" H and 4.75" W with the wings closed. $85-125. (Other colors are valued much less.)

Male Chauvinist Pig is an AM radio shaped like a pig. The pink pig has a curly tail which functions as the off/on control. The words "Male Chauvinist PIG" are printed on the side of the pig's rump. This radio was made in Hong Kong and measures 9" L. $35-60.

Mortar and Pestle is an AM radio made in Japan. This radio is shaped like a mortar and pestle with the raised printing "*malmonides*" and "*secundum*" decorating it. There is also a raised figure of a man in the center. This radio was made for the medicine "Coricidan." It stands 6.5" H. $45-70.

Notebook, Young 6 is an AM radio shaped like a red notebook. There is a small, tuner window on the front with "Toshiba"® printed under it. This radio came with a case. It measures 5" H, 3" W, and 1" thick. $25-40.

LOVE IS … a two-dimensional radio made in Hong Kong. The radio pictures nude girl and boy figures holding a ball. The radio says " Love is … for us." It measures 5" H and 6.5" L, and has an attached carrying strap. $30-55.

Rock is an AM/FM radio of unknown origin. It is a plastic radio shaped like a square rock. It has a large speaker in the center and is colored black with white specks. This radio measures 5.5" L. $20-35.

Seahorse is an AM/FM radio shaped like a seahorse. The changes the radio from AM to FM and the eye controls the volume. The fin on the seahorse changes the station and there are speaker holes in the stomach. $25-40.

Panda Bears is an AM radio. It looks like an alarm clock with two pandas in the center. This radio is 4.25" H. $15-35.

Penguin Shower radio is molded plastic in the shape of a penguin. The penguin is standing on one foot and is wearing a mask and a life preserver. This radio is common. $15-25.

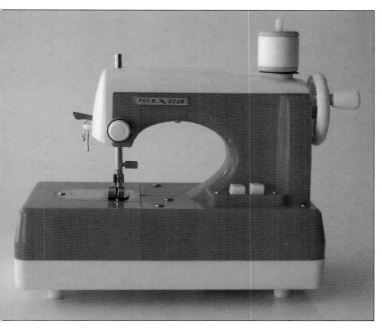

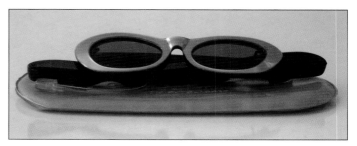

Sunglasses is an unusual looking radio. The sunglasses have short wires on the sides with small speakers attached. When these sunglasses are worn, the wire-ends are inserted in the ears. This radio was made in Hong Kong and came with a pink plastic case. The sunglasses are 8" L. $35-50.

Sewing Machine is an AM radio made in Japan. This radio also functions as a sewing machine. There is a hand-crank on the back that moves the needle when turned. This radio measures 8" L. $60-80.

Suitcase is an AM/FM radio. It is shaped like a suitcase with wheels that turn. It even has a handle on the top. This radio was made in China and is 4.5" H. $15-25.

Talking Dolphin is a scanner-type radio made in China. It is shaped like a dolphin standing on a black base. This radio has a yellow switch on the base that will activate the dolphin's mouth to move. $20-35.

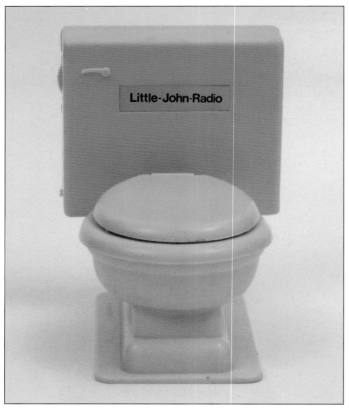

Troll is a molded plastic radio made in China. This radio has an antenna inside the tall pink hair. Thumbwheels control the volume and tuning. $25-40.

Toilet, Little John, is shaped like a toilet. This radio is yellow and white, but there are many other colors available. The tank on the toilet has a sign that says "Little John Radio." This radio was made in Hong Kong and came in a box shaped like a roll of toilet paper. It measures 4.25" H and 4.25" L. $20-35.

Toilet, Outhouse, radio is made in the shape of a wooden outhouse. The radio is plastic and is pictured with the door opened. If inspected closely, a Sears® catalog can be seen hanging inside the outhouse. The front of the door has a crescent moon cutout. This radio is 5.5" H and was made in Japan. It is dated 1971. $35-50.

Tune-A-Bear is an AM radio made in Hong Kong. This is one of a series of many different "Tune-A" radios. This radio is shaped like a smiling bear wearing a red tie. The tuning and volume controls are behind the ears. This radio is 7.5" H. $15-30.

Tune-A-Hound is another AM radio from the "Tune-A" series. It is shaped like a dog with long ears wearing a crocheted hat. The dog's cheeks have speaker holes in them. This radio is 6.5" H. $15-30.

Tune-A-Monkey is another AM radio from the "Tune-A" series. It is shaped like a monkey wearing a pink suit and hat. This radio was made in Hong Kong and stands 7" H. $15-30.

Tune-A-Leo is another AM radio from the "Tune-A" series. It was made in Hong Kong and stands 5.5" H. This radio is shaped like a lion, who appears to be looking up. It has an attached carrying strap. $15-30.

Tune-A-Pig is another AM radio from the "Tune-A" series. It was made in Hong Kong and is only 4" H. This radio is shaped like a pig. The pig has vinyl ears that can be lifted, exposing the volume and tuning controls. $15-30.

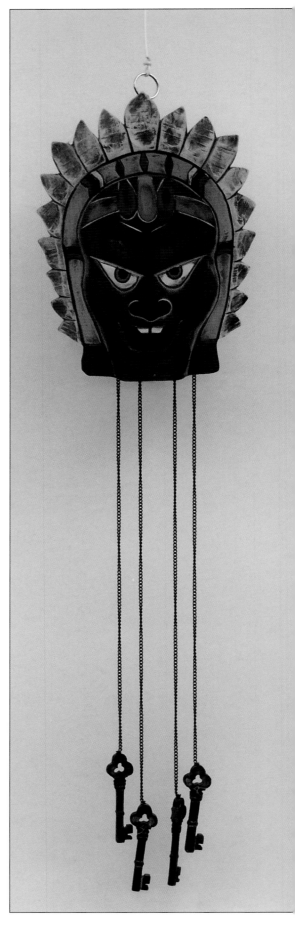

Wooden Indian is an unusual looking radio. It is shaped like a head wearing a feathered headdress. The Indian has large, fierce-looking eyes and two top teeth in his opened mouth. The side of the radio has a metal plate attached. The plate contains a sliding tuner and the words "6 Transistor, Monarch, Made in Japan." There are four keys attached to four long chains on the bottom of the radio. The chains control the tuning and volume. $50-75.

Index